Code to Commerce

Code to Commerce

High Technology Marketing for Maximum Brand Performance

First Edition

Wm. Edward Vesely

Writers Club Press
San Jose New York Lincoln Shanghai

Code to Commerce
High Technology Marketing for Maximum Brand Performance

Writers Club Press
an imprint of iUniverse, Inc.

For information address:
iUniverse, Inc.
5220 S. 16th St., Suite 200
Lincoln, NE 68512
www.iuniverse.com

ISBN: 0-595-24690-7

Printed in the United States of America

To my daughter, Amanda.

Remember that the brave may not live forever,
but the cautious do not live at all. Always seek the impossible,
which is never more than a step away.

Contents

Preface

As a veteran high technology marketing professional, I have lived through the very best—and worst—of recent times.

Investor and employee alike now understand that the high technology boon of the 90s was not based on financial fundamentals. Neither was it based on solid business plans or market dominance or product superiority. This boon was the result of unprecedented hype and emotion that surreptitiously found its way to venture capital, day trader and mutual fund stockpiles.

Even senior venture capitalists and investment bankers, many of whom are known for their business prowess, allowed inexperienced armchair finance and marketing rookies to unduly influence their decisions, and ultimately, the decisions of well-intentioned boards of directors. There was simply too much occurring too fast for any reasonable level of control. Spin doctors and sound bites ruled the day.

And then the bubble burst. Hundreds of thousands of layoffs occurred and broken dreams were scattered across the global high technology landscape.

Code to Commerce is written for senior business and marketing professionals who want to make a difference. Individuals who want to achieve breakthrough results, and understand that they must first develop a strategic plan and staying power to achieve market dominance.

It occurred to me while taking a company through its initial public offering that most high technology business professionals don't actually know how to go from "code to commerce." They don't understand the commercialization process that companies must navigate in order to achieve success. The same principles that apply to all industries, whether large or small, clicks or bricks.

Code to Commerce, written in handbook format, provides a rare look at marketing best practices that add lasting value to brands and the stakeholders that rely on them. It is a high technology marketing sourcebook that can be used from war room to boardroom:

- It provides refreshing and insightful experience for high technology business professionals who are under constant fire to produce.
- It motivates readers and challenges their current assumptions.
- It explains specific strategies and techniques regarding the commercialization process that companies must navigate in order to succeed.

Yes, marketing books fill the shelves. Many convey generalities and interesting stories that make good cocktail party material, but provide little value to serious business professionals who are under pressure to perform. *Code to Commerce* is the first practical resource that fills this void and addresses how high technology business and marketing professionals can achieve commercial success.

To borrow a line from a successful rock band, "if you're tired of the same old story, turn some pages." I hope that you find the journey to be an energizing and profitable use of your time.

Chasm or Spasm?

This is an exciting time to be in business. Change is accelerating at unparalleled levels. Technology-enabled sales and marketing is allowing small businesses to gain global recognition, while large enterprises are becoming smaller and more intimate with their customers and other stakeholders.

Yes, the digital age is exploding, and successful businesses and marketers are not only capitalizing on it, but are in fact leading the revolution. Each telephone call, purchase transaction and electronic tollbooth crossing is being registered and analyzed. And information has become the currency of our era as it impacts organizational strategy and behavior for decades to come.

While business has been busy implementing e-business, enterprise resource planning and supply chain systems, the technological focus on marketing is relatively new—and less understood. But that is changing. In fact, leading analyst organizations continue to predict staggering growth rates for technology-enabled sales and marketing solutions that promise to radically change the way organizations behave, improve financial performance and increase customer satisfaction.

Why such growth? Well, business leaders continue to cite improving services for customers, reducing costs and increasing profits as being among their top business objectives. Consequently, corporate investment in marketing is steadily increasing as business leaders view marketing as a strategic financial investment, rather than an expense.

But with investment comes accountability and responsibility. Leading marketing organizations recognize the need to meet the financial and other objectives of their primary stakeholders—customers, corporate management and employees, shareholders and communities at large. And professional marketers now recognize that they are accountable to their constituents and responsible for their performance.

Code to Commerce provides unique insight into the world of high stakes, technology-enabled marketing. But perhaps more importantly, *Code to Commerce* helps you—marketing, sales and other business professionals—establish a proven marketing platform that has delivered breakthrough results in extremely harsh business conditions. In fact, these flexible, resilient methods have been developed and refined in the most competitive global high technology environments.

Experienced marketers know that successful integrated marketing begins with the buyer. Understanding buyer values enables organizations to gain critical insights that result in satisfied repeat customers, market share and increasingly important wallet share.

An interesting and entertaining read is Geoffrey Moore's *Crossing the Chasm*. However, the difficulty that many business and marketing professionals have with the text is that most companies are not in the enviable situation where printing product CDs fast enough is their major challenge. Today's era of one-to-one marketing and relationship selling requires new skills and thinking. It's not volume, but a continuous and renewable chain of value that keeps leading companies in front.

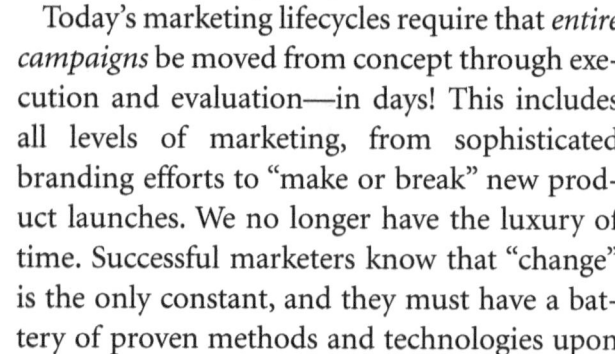

Today's marketing lifecycles require that *entire campaigns* be moved from concept through execution and evaluation—in days! This includes all levels of marketing, from sophisticated branding efforts to "make or break" new product launches. We no longer have the luxury of time. Successful marketers know that "change" is the only constant, and they must have a battery of proven methods and technologies upon which they can rely. Without proven marketing methods and strategies, today's marketers and their businesses are predestined for failure—it is simply a matter of time.

Each aspect of high technology marketing—from electronic to paper, public relations to advertising, direct mail to Internet—must be viewed with the buyer in mind, and must speak to specific buyer values or it is simply worthless. And worse yet, it can cost valuable time and opportunity that may result in unrecoverable circumstances.

Performance Marketing

Introduction

Though the Performance Marketing Lifecycle that is introduced in this book has been developed in the most challenging high technology marketing environments, its principles apply to every major business-to-business and business-to-consumer industry. As a result, this flexible and proven methodology should guide you through the creation and execution of your marketing plans, regardless of your professional background, industry or experience. And since the methodology encourages input from various functional units within the organization, it naturally serves as a common framework for collaboration among business professionals from marketing, sales, finance and other disciplines.

It is important that marketing professionals are both creative and analytical in their approach to developing their marketing plans. Gone are the days when marketing professionals could rely solely on their creative talents to gain the credibility they needed to be successful. Today, integrated marketing professionals are more "business than creative" and are able to clearly analyze the marketing return on investment for a company, division or campaign.

Performance Marketing is not based on rigid formulas or hypothetical models, but instead is a flexible roadmap that is customized to ensure that situational strategies and tactics are incorporated. As a result, these best practices provide unique benefits:

- All plans are created using similar steps which enable an organization to develop cross-functional marketing expertise, best practices and nomenclature.
- Performance Marketing provides a common approach for implementing marketing plans and programs across many businesses, industries and markets.

- This business-based approach ensures that marketers are in alignment with broader corporate objectives and strategies.
- Common review points increase quality and efficiency, minimize expensive mistakes and ensure cross functional "buy in."

Finally, adopting the Performance Marketing approach enhances the quality of your final business and marketing plans, and improves communication throughout the entire enterprise. And it enables marketing professionals to contribute at the most senior levels—from the boardroom through executive row.

Four Cs of Performance Marketing

Many of us are familiar with the "Four Ps" of marketing—product, place, price and promotion. While its creator was triumphant in advancing marketing as a disciplined profession, the definition alone is relatively primitive in an era where marketing is increasingly viewed as a strategic initiative in virtually every corporate war room.

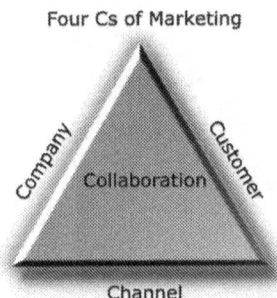

Four Cs of Marketing

Advancing this concept, *Code to Commerce* introduces the "Four Cs" of marketing—company, customer, channel and collaboration—that must be thoroughly examined and addressed in the new era of strategic marketing. Addressing these four elements elevates marketing to strategic, breakthrough levels, as opposed to the more tactical Four Ps which continue to be relevant as elements of a Four C program. Performance Marketing, the proven approach that is outlined in this book, builds extensively on this concept.

The *company* is of course the "producing and selling" institution, which may in fact be multiple distinct organizations. In our increasingly virtual world, the company may be comprised of a network of smaller businesses, many of which are not known to the customer. The more complex the product and channel, the more likely it is that intermediaries will maintain the closest relationships with customers. This is especially true in the business-to-business world in which dealers, service centers and retailers represent manufacturers—and therefore have substantial influence on their brands and relationships with customers.

The company model will change dramatically across industries and geographies. Over time, the most successful structure will be the one that delivers the greatest value and customer satisfaction with the least cost. It will be the one with which customers find it easiest to conduct business, while maintaining efficiency, resilience and the ability to react quickly to market demands and changes.

The *customer* is the person and the many characteristics that make him what he is. His position, role and charter within his organization. His beliefs, values and personal attributes, and his demographic and socioeconomic portrait. The customer is the supreme being within our stakeholder world. Without this omnipotent element, the rest of the ecosystem simply fails.

In this virtual, multi-channel world, it is increasingly important—and difficult—to understand and stay connected with customers.

Purchasing models vary widely, and companies continue to struggle for ways to understand, acquire and maintain valuable customers.

Enter the *channel*. This is the world that many marketing professionals fail to understand as they leap from A to Z—going from the basic need to market a product or service, to initiating a full blown advertising campaign—without adequately considering the interim phases that accelerate value and generate lifelong customer relationships. The optimum channel is the means to most efficiently and effectively collaborate with customers and enter into meaningful relationships.

Each industry has its own channels which are ultimately determined by buyer values and preferences. Whether a company chooses to direct market, leverage dealers and distributors, or some combination, technology will continue to play an important role in helping companies maintain efficient relationships with channel partners and customers.

Finally, *collaboration*. There has been so much written about collaboration that it is important to put a framework around it for our purposes. Collaboration is the interaction that we maintain with our customers, channel partners and other stakeholders, and the ensuing relationships that develop. Certainly we are interested in moving from interaction to transaction, but it is in the interaction-transaction-interaction events that generate true viral market power.

This is where technology again enters into our discussion. Performance Marketing professionals have more high quality, low cost technology at their beckon call than at any other time in history. We will examine some of these technologies in a subsequent chapter. For now, let us assume that technology-enabled sales and marketing solutions are sufficiently available to facilitate profitable collaboration between companies, customers and channel members.

Performance Marketing Process

Performance Marketing plays a central role in the development of any good or service. Whether you have a role with a software or hardware, service or finance organization, you have a moral and financial obligation to each and every stakeholder—employees, customers, partners, investors and the community at large—to invest limited resources that have been entrusted to you in such a way that maximum returns are realized in appropriate time frames.

Performance Marketing begins with the customer; the buyer who most influences your organization and gives it a reason to exist. Performance Marketing professionals understand that buyer values are the keys to success; the gateways to efficiencies and strategies that result in accelerated growth and market dominance.

Have you ever wondered how a failed product ever made it to market? Whether the automotive engineer actually drove his poorly-designed car or the programmer ever used his own software? I remember listening to a software company president instruct his development organization that they must begin to use their own software, when one naïve programmer raised his hand and proclaimed "but, it's difficult to use!"

The point is that regardless of our role, we must be responsible for our own actions toward exceeding customer expectations. We often need to be reminded that we are in business for customers, that buyer values determine what we produce and that we will be out of business if we do not respond to their call. It is that simple.

The most efficient and effective ways to reach your customer and collaborate through his preferred contact points must be fully understood before effective marketing strategies and programs can be designed and implemented. In the global world of business-to-business marketing, channel programs can become quite complex as multi-tiered direct sales forces engage alongside retailers, resellers, service centers and

Internet-based selling systems. The challenge for Performance Marketing professionals is to develop and maintain a consistent, yet powerful brand that can be leveraged across multiple channels to impart the ultimate buying experience.

Performance Marketing Platform

The Performance Marketing Platform builds upon five simple elements which are thoroughly discussed in subsequent chapters.

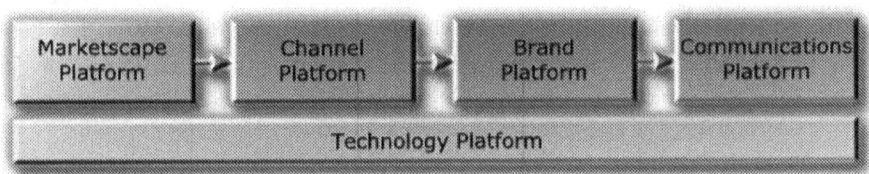

Marketscape Platform

During the initial phase of the Performance Marketing Lifecycle, buyers are fully analyzed and understood, and elements of the Marketscape Platform can be examined in context. This includes internal elements such as corporate objectives, competencies and deficiencies. And external influences such as political and economic conditions, competitors and market trends are also analyzed.

A fully developed Marketscape Platform provides keen insight as to the best possible means of taking your product or service to market.

Channel Platform

Multiple channels—direct and indirect—are often needed to reach and support buyers in the most expedient, efficient and profitable manner. The integration of various processes, business rules and technologies must therefore be carefully considered.

If a buyer chooses to research your product on the Internet, purchase it at a local retail store and have it supported at a local service center, your channel strategy must support this without depreciating your brand or the customer experience in any way. The Channel Platform chapter fully develops this concept that is rarely considered in published marketing works. Along with buyer values, brand strategy is also a major focus in this phase of your marketing lifecycle.

Brand Platform

Developing a Brand Platform requires an intimate knowledge of organizational objectives, buyer values and channel requirements. That is, the Brand Platform directly follows and supports the findings of the Marketscape and Channel Platforms. Brand management in the digital age is among the most valuable long-term practices that an organization can undertake.

Whether or not your brand equity is directly recognized on your balance sheet (e.g., as it may be in England), Performance Marketing professionals understand the importance of developing a valuable, well-architected brand. The Brand Platform chapter explores the many issues and options that must be considered when developing a successful brand hierarchy.

Communications Platform

And now enters the Communications Platform. How many times has someone, perhaps an inexperienced board member, recommended that you simply "run some ads?"

"Specifically, what type of campaign?" you reply.
- "Whom should it target? What are their buying values?
- Should it be feature-, value- or quality-based?
- Testimony, product comparison or case study oriented?
- Print or electronic? What does the buyer prefer?

- Should it be integrated with the other elements of the sales and marketing process? Direct mail and email? Web? Telemarketing? Events?
- What's the budget?
- What is the expected response and how should it be measured?
- And finally, are YOU (Mr. Board Member) willing to take responsibility for the results?"

Establishing a proactive, smart and flexible Communications Platform gives you options that you will need as you conduct marketing warfare on behalf of your stakeholders. It enables you to behave aggressively, adapt quickly and measure responsibly—with little waste and inefficiency. The Communications Platform chapter fully explores the strategic considerations and implications of a winning execution program.

Technology Platform

The Technology Platform is the combination of technology-enabled sales and marketing solutions that are implemented to support the entire Performance Marketing Lifecycle. It is this platform that provides lasting value and economies of scale that enable companies to realize benefits and results in time frames that were previously not possible.

Traditional product lifecycles have given way to the accelerated product innovation, launch, adoption and retirement cycles that have become commonplace. This is due in part to the penetration, adoption and pervasiveness of technology throughout virtually every major market and economy.

EZ Commerce, Inc.

Finally, *Code to Commerce* utilizes a formal case study for EZ Commerce, a fictional e-business software company. The founder of EZ Commerce chose its name because, as a technologist, he believed his technology would simply "fly off the shelves."

Listed on the NASDAQ exchange, EZ Commerce is headquartered in San Jose, with regional offices throughout the United States and Western Europe. The company is also considering partnerships that would facilitate its entry in Asia-Pacific.

EZ Commerce develops, markets and supports a suite of e-business software that facilitates sell-side business-to-business and business-to-consumer e-commerce. The EZ Software Series enables a manufacturer's channel partners and consumers to purchase products and services in a highly personalized, secure Internet environment.

EZ Commerce has a direct sales force, and intends to develop indirect channels that can support its exponential growth objectives, which translate to "software flying off shelves."

More on EZ Commerce as our case study unfolds.

Marketscape Platform

Most players tend to play where the puck is,
whereas I play where the puck is going to be.
Wayne Gretzky

Near the turn of this century, during the great dot com IPO rush, scores of high technology companies that were being driven by their boards and often inexperienced, yet powerful, venture capitalists:

- Crafted half-baked vision statements with broad supporting statements and showcased flawed marketing intelligence that claimed to know what their buyers valued and where their markets where going;
- Hired thousands of highly paid professionals in virtually every area of their businesses;
- Retained expensive sales, marketing, branding, executive search and "strategic" business consulting agencies;
- Developed, announced and launched immature products that offered little value and had almost no staying power;
- And even received billions of dollars in venture funding—without being able to clearly articulate their core competencies, vision, market potential or time-to-profitability!

This, of course, was a primary reason for the NASDAQ's technology sector crash in early 2000. There simply wasn't enough value being created—and the market dropped more than 70 percent in 12 months. History, of course, has a way of repeating itself. Performance Marketing practices ensure that you are operating from a game plan that is based on sound business principles—regardless of the economic climate.

Assess the Current Environment

The environmental assessment portion of your Marketscape Platform considers three essential factors that will be continually revisited: business strategy, technology and marketing. As a business and marketing professional, you will need to develop a keen understanding of each factor.

You should minimally consider your competitive landscape, and your ability to close in on a market—in a collapsed timeframe. What are your competencies? How do they compare with your competition? Can you deliver product on time? Will your product's benefits surpass and be more evident than those that have gone before you? Can you quickly gain mind share and do you have financial staying power?

And don't forget revenue. Your investors—whether Wall Street market makers or venture capitalists—are extremely unforgiving. One misstep or inability to execute—especially in the early stages of brand development, and you could find that your dreams are sacrificed and you are simply not able to recover.

It is therefore essential that you, as a strategic marketing professional, conduct a realistic inventory of your company's core business competencies. What skills will you need to grow or acquire? And what are the gaps between market expectations for your product or service and your ability to deliver?

Of course you have several options for narrowing these gaps—the "build, buy or partner" alternatives—should you choose to address one or more shortcomings. You may not be able to attend to them all, but instead will need to determine where to spend precious resources. It has been said that life is a series of compromises. This process will be no different for you and your organization.

And what about the environmental factors that will affect your ability to succeed? Certainly there are always competitive pressures, but you should become accustomed to channeling your responses to actually capitalize on them. Competition can be healthy as it brings out our best capitalistic energies and results.

You should also review the geopolitical factors that could affect your ability to succeed, and be prepared for the occurrence of likely scenarios. Crisis management and scenario planning are baseline skills for strategic marketing professionals of this era.

Other environmental factors to consider include economic trends such as the availability of capital or the overall health of the economy. If outside capital is not sufficiently available to rapidly expand your direct sales channel, for instance, you may find that partnering models offer more potential. This scenario may also result in you establishing distribution partnerships for both defensive and offensive reasons.

Social trends can also affect an organization—favorably or adversely. For instance, if consumers are not ready for a product or service due to prevailing ideological beliefs, you may choose to repackage your offering or wait until the climate changes.

Of course there are countless other environmental factors including changing demographics and political landscapes that can affect your ability to succeed during a given moment in time. Progressive crisis management and scenario planning practices can anticipate and even capitalize on even the most unfortunate change in events.

Create a Compelling Vision

A company vision should first and foremost speak to its customer stakeholders. Period. Understanding their behaviors, preferences, buying habits and needs are cornerstone to any serious business plan or company vision.

You need to motivate each of your stakeholders to participate in your future by clearly articulating your aspirations and compelling them to action. In doing so, you need to paint a vision in which people want to take part. The vision should be constructed and clearly articulated by senior management, and consistently communicated by each employee.

Market Segmentation

Appropriately segmenting your buyers is one of the most important phases in the entire integrated marketing lifecycle. Without understanding market characteristics and segment sizes, buyer values and behaviors, and buyer preferences such as preferred contact points, your marketing efforts are doomed. No amount of technology, marketing prowess or luck will sustain you long term if you have not addressed this first.

Market Sizing

Once you have segmented your markets, how do you go about sizing them? Fortunately for the Performance Marketing professional, there are proven methods available to assist in the process of calculating the size of markets and their respective growth rates.

You'll need to determine market size through traditional means that include:

- Simple Trend Analysis—Review historical data and use the rates of change to project future trends.

- Market Share Analysis—Assume that your market share will remain constant, and then project future sales at the industry growth rate.
- Test Marketing—When there are no historical data, you will need to introduce products into test markets and document the results.
- Market Consolidation—Estimate the size of other segments using one of the other techniques, and aggregate them.
- Market Breakdown—The opposite of consolidation, you begin with the industry, the largest players, etc., and then break it down to extrapolate your share.
- Salesperson Estimates—Estimate the number of units and/or revenue that can be sold through an individual sales person, then aggregate for the entire sales force with room for error.
- Other methods such as statistical analysis and a variety of marketing focus groups can be leveraged to arrive at meaningful segment and market sizing.

You should familiarize yourself with these straightforward methods for calculating market size and share. You might also find that relevant research is available from one of the many industry analyst groups who gather, analyze and publish data and information.

Customer Buyer Values

Once this is accomplished, you need to identify the individual buyers and their respective buyer values within each of these segments. It is essential that the *individual buyer* be considered as the target market in this process, as you will need to carry this information throughout the entire integrated marketing lifecycle.

For instance, EZ Commerce has found that business and information technology buyers of its e-commerce solution value the following characteristics:

Business buyers want to:
- Respond to change
- Create competitive advantage
- Improve channel relationships
- Reduce expenses
- Adopt easy-to-use products
- Increase revenue
- Increase industry vertical competency

IT buyers want solutions that:
- Are comprehensive, integrated
- Leverage their IT investment
- Are mission critical
- Are scalable and extensible
- Reduce deployment complexity

Ultimately, there are a variety of ways to segment your customers and prospects. In doing so, you might choose to adopt one of these simple categorization models:
- Loyal installed base, competitive installed base or emerging buyers,
- Loyal buyers, switchers or new prospects,
- Compliers, complainers or inquirers, or
- Purchasers, recommenders or evaluators.

What are their behaviors? Their individual values? And how can you most efficiently and effectively reach them? Properly segmenting your customer base is one of the most important activities you can undertake. Understanding their behaviors and values will determine the messages to create, distribution channels to develop and "whole" products to create and package. It will also enable you to determine the appropriate:
- Marketing communications and public relations programs to execute,
- Product launch strategies and techniques,
- Brand development strategies, and
- Cross selling and product development strategies.

Once you have determined the correct buyer values and behaviors, you'll need to identify the best ways to reach your individual customers and prospects. Multiple technologies exist to help you reach them in a concerted manner, but you'll first need to examine external touch points and ensure that you are maximizing each and every encounter to your customers' ultimate satisfaction.

While you are examining these external touch points, take advantage of the opportunity to audit whether your brand is being consistently and properly represented along the entire chain of stakeholder contact points—with customers, corporate managers and other employees, shareholders and communities.

Competitive Analysis

As you conduct formal analyses of your competitors, you should consider all facets of their business to determine their relative health. Companies are organisms. They can fall ill, but they can also recover quickly given the right assets—and market timing.

Performance Marketing competitive analysis functions evaluate the following *business dimensions* in order to effectively assess and understand the competition:

- Business and financial position—The length of time in business, location of sales offices, development labs and corporate offices, financial position and staying power, primary investors and noteworthy events such as recent strategic acquisitions.
- Customer base—The demographic makeup of their customers, with particular attention being paid to the various industry verticals that have been penetrated.
- Solution (product or service)—The offering, ways it is packaged, how it is priced, and in the case of a high technology product, other products, technologies and services that are used to produce the solution.
- Sales and channel model—The primary and secondary channels that are used to reach buyers, the leading partners in each model and the type of partner (e.g., distribution, integration, technology, etc.).

- Marketing strategies and programs—The types of press releases that have been issued, slogans in use, branding and co-branding techniques and an analysis of each marketing communication element from collateral and Web content to events, advertising, direct marketing and public relations.
- *Their SWOT*—Your competitors' strengths, weaknesses, opportunities and perceived threats. It is difficult yet important to consider these from their perspective. If you were in their position, what would be your next move?

Interview their customers. Hire their best sales and support people. Do whatever it takes—in accelerated time frames—to secure the information you need to leapfrog your competitors in their areas of strength.

Do not focus solely on their weakness. This is a common trap of nearly all junior marketers. Their strengths were developed because the market drove them there! You must be better than your competitors in their key areas of competency. Once the market learns this, and understands that you also provide other substantial benefits, your brand will thrive.

Describe the Market Opportunity

Never "shoot the arrow first and then paint the target" regardless of the pressure that you are under from stakeholders that might include your CEO and board of directors. And you must flee the deadly practice of making the numbers agree with your plan. You will only be deceiving your employees, shareholders—and ultimately yourself.

Instead, do your homework, identify a viable market and develop a business plan that can succeed on its own merits. And if you are not planning to grow at a rate equal to or greater than the industry, then find a new business. Period. Competition is simply too fierce to justify half-hearted attempts at growing the business.

A final note on demand forecasting, which is both art and science. You need a thorough understanding of the different sales and channel models in place to build your own forecasting model. And you should include three important areas in your revenue model: acquiring new customers, extending the duration of customer relationships and enhancing the profitability of existing customers.

Successful Performance Marketing professionals will consider each of these three goals in developing their integrated strategic marketing plans. In the early phases of an emerging organization's lifecycle, acquiring new customers might be the primary focus.

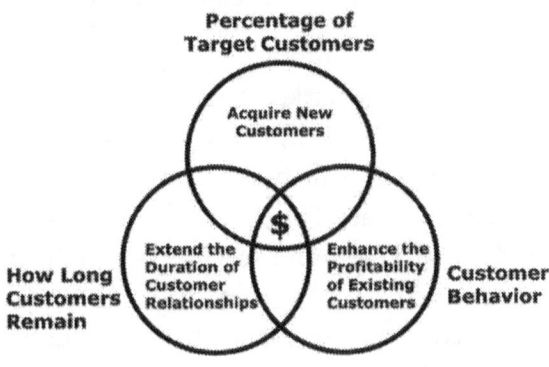

As you look toward maximizing your valuation, a shift may ultimately occur as you demonstrate your ability to maintain satisfied, lifetime customers. And your marketing information systems must also be in place to effectively monitor and understand customer behavior so that you can be sure of a solid recurring revenue stream.

It is at this point that you gather the information you have collected, begin to prepare a professional brief and presentation, and get ready to meet with executive management—but not until you have documented viable market entry options, scenarios and recommendations. This brief should clearly communicate early considerations that can be developed during subsequent Channel and Brand Platform definition phases—and beyond.

Four Cs of Marketing In Action

During the Marketscape Platform phase, it is essential that we accurately identify buyer values, in order to benchmark how we can actually exceed customer expectations.

EZ Commerce Marketscape Platform

EZ Commerce hired a strategic marketing consulting firm to assist it in developing a Marketscape Platform. Remember, the company develops, markets and supports a suite of e-business software that facilitates sell-side business-to-business and business-to-consumer e-commerce. The EZ Software Series enables channel partners and consumers to purchase products and services in a highly personalized, secure Internet environment.

The company began with a thorough analysis of the competitive offerings that were being offered. This analysis considered the dimensions described earlier: business and financial position, customer base, product or service, sales and channel model, marketing strategies and programs, and each competitors' SWOT.

After speaking with a number of customers, EZ Commerce determined that buyers most often grouped these competitive solutions into one or more of the following segments:

- Complete, end-to-end offerings that were being offered by industry gorillas.
- Integration solutions that would enable a new e-commerce application to communicate with a customer's existing order entry, financial and shipping systems, or communicate with a channel partner or customer through an e-commerce portal.
- Point products that enhanced an e-commerce application with features such as personalization, security or content management.
- Platform solutions that provided a working environment with which to build a complete e-commerce solution.

Each of these segments was described with distinct characteristics that defined its uniqueness and commonality. For instance, EZ Commerce learned that its rapid implementation capabilities were a unique value to customers, and compared this to their competitors' abilities to provide more complete solutions in the following diagram:

Marketscape Segmentation Map

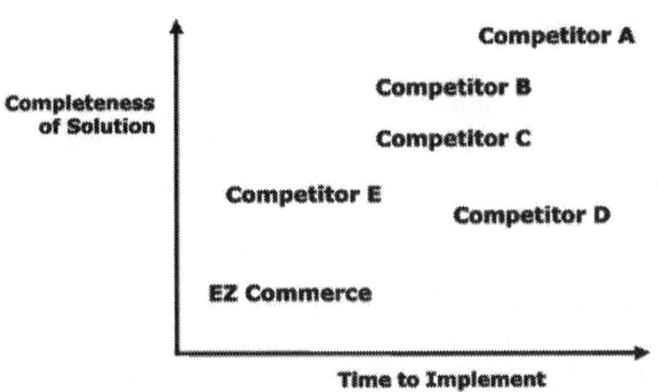

By summarizing its findings in this way, EZ Commerce marketing management was able to quickly communicate to executive management its primary relative strength (i.e., rapid implementation) and weakness (i.e., simple solution).

EZ Commerce began to see that it was not going to be quite so "easy" after all. As a result of its extensive data gathering and analysis, the marketing department was able to report the following findings:

- Marketing segmentation—A convergence was rapidly underway among all segments studied, leading to intense competition and price pressure.
- Business and financial position—Investors were already spending large sums in this segment, resulting in well-funded competitors with significant staying power. Markets were already maturing,

many established players were dominating each of the dimensions studied and the rapid consolidation of companies was underway.

- Solution—While individual competitors' approaches may differ, the implemented results of their solutions are generally similar. The rapid implementation approach and vertical industry expertise could be a unique differentiator.
- Technology—Java, XML and open standards/architectures were beginning to dominate, with standards body participation becoming key to establishing credibility. Wireless technology was becoming the new wave.
- Marketing strategies and programs—Technology-focused go-to-market strategies dominated. Expansive, elegant "marketecture" was essential to simplifying complex architectures and solutions. Some vendors demonstrated keen branding expertise.
- Sales and channel model—Success appeared to lie in the channels where established relationships were already in place. OEM, technology and service relationships dominated.
- Customer base—Vendors already had diversified "brand name" client bases, and non-U.S. markets were also being targeted and penetrated.

Independent, third party research can be a valuable source of input to your Marketscape Platform analysis. Industry analyst firms such as Gartner, IDC, Meta Group, Forrester Research and Yankee Group publish research and analysis for organizations such as EZ Commerce and its customers. For instance, by utilizing this research, EZ Commerce was able to analyze the projected e-business spending for its solution by industry.

As a result of its research, EZ Commerce decided to adopt a "viral" beachhead marketing approach, whereby it would:

- Focus on winning and protecting an attractive niche.
- Step up its promotion as the leading solution provider in that niche.

- Begin to position for subsequent niches with new vertical and functional offerings.
- Begin to prepare for additional geographic penetration.
- Lead product expansion efforts with marketing activities.
- And quickly develop regional sales capabilities after demand has been demonstrated in the market.

In order to maximize its marketing investment, EZ Commerce further decided to integrate all marketing and product plans for maximum effect. Realizing it was a relative newcomer compared to the more established players, EZ Commerce committed the company to expanding its industry, product and international presence using a simple, pragmatic approach. As a result, the steps that EZ Commerce took to expand in each area are outlined below:

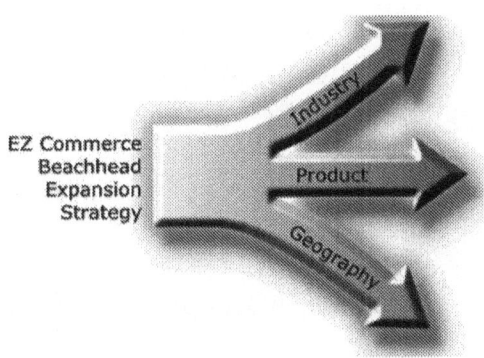

Industry breadth—EZ Commerce established four simple steps for industry penetration:
1. Identify and prioritize high potential industries.

2. Specify sales/consulting teams for each target vertical.
3. Develop white papers for industry verticals and specific functional areas.
4. Investigate potential acquisitions.

Product breadth—EZ Commerce's executive team determined to expand its product capabilities in the following way:
1. Continue to broaden the EZ Software Series solution.
2. Actively market EZ Commerce as a leader in the initial product niche.

International expansion—Finally, EZ Commerce established a pragmatic geographic expansion plan, which included the following:
1. Evaluate the current plan.
2. Identify potential seed clients.
3. Explore distribution "franchises" as an alternative to substantial incremental EZ Commerce investment.

At this stage of the lifecycle, market entry options or dimensions should be clearly documented for products and services that are being considered for introduction. For instance, EZ Commerce examined the following options for bringing to market its e-commerce product or expanding its offering into new markets:
- Enter with a "quick sale" low-price offer.
- Enter with an established player (e.g., a complementary, established mid-market ERP vendor).
- Enter in another geographic market where competition is not yet established (e.g., outside North America where U.S. competitors are not yet mature).
- Cross-sell across its existing client base.
- Enter as a "breakthrough architecture" solution (e.g., architected for wireless e-business).

- Develop or acquire industry expertise to broaden the solution offering, raise the price, enter other verticals, etc.

The company then assessed the levels of difficulty and resource that must be applied to each option, as depicted in the following graphic:

Dimensional Entry Comparison

Difficulty of Each Growth Dimension

And finally, EZ Commerce considered the relative opportunity of each option and weighed the costs accordingly:

Dimensional Growth Compared

Growth Opportunity Assessment

Once these findings were complete and the models were developed, the marketing department was in a position to begin the important and relatively unique Channel Platform phase.

Channel Platform

If you want loyalty, buy a dog.

Today's selling machines come in a surplus of sizes and shapes. However, the decision to implement a particular model should be driven primarily by the customer, the cost/benefit ratio, your overall ability to execute and your product's corresponding level of quality and maturity.

For instance, if both your product and buyer require a solution-oriented, consultative sales approach, then you'll need to integrate industry experts into the sales cycle. Perhaps your ideal buyer is a senior executive—then you might consider inside sales or telemarketing as a way to establish initial contact—and avoid other costly marketing programs. Or you might choose to leverage senior industry spokespersons, board members, executive seminars or high-end direct marketing programs as a means of gaining access to executive ranks.

Regardless, before you are able to develop an effective channel platform, you should be able to clearly articulate answers to these questions:
- What does the buyer really want? Not the product or service, but the end result for the business.
- How can you best reach him?
- How "simple and easy" or "complex and difficult" is your product to sell?
- How much evangelism and education must be completed on the market category before you are able to present your specific solution?

- What is the expected productivity of each sales person—in net dollars—and what is the cost and time to get him up to speed and fully productive?
- How long will it take you to get a sales force in place and productive in the industry verticals and geographies that you are targeting?
- And how can partnerships and alliances help you achieve your market penetration and revenue goals?

Alliances and partnerships are radically changing the sales and marketing competitive landscape in virtually every industry. Those organizations with an effective, well-founded channel plan stand a good chance of succeeding, yet ineffective plans can have disastrous, fatiguing effects and result in missed opportunities.

Key business drivers fueling today's flurry of channel activity include converging technologies that often require companies to collaborate with global partners. Escalating research and development costs can cause companies to align, and deciding that it is more economical to buy than to build products and components can also drive partnership strategies.

Other drivers include seeking access to new markets, which open and close quickly. And acquiring new customers can also require indirect channels, as can supporting customers in distant or remote regions.

Supporting Whole Product Requirements

Any serious channel discussion should begin with the customer's "whole product" requirements. That is, the combination of product and service that will result in the highest degree of success in the marketplace. Only when the requirements have been identified and documented—by surveying customers and channel players, and conducting extensive market and competitive research—should you begin to assess the readiness of your product in meeting the market's requirements.

It is in the gaps—the areas in which you are not able to meet market expectations—that you should first consider alliances or partnerships to fill the voids. Of course there are other factors, such as the relative cost and opportunity or gain that will also weigh heavily in this process.

Another important technique to consider in this process is to "value weight" customer and market expectations and needs for the requirements that they have set. You should then assess the corresponding readiness of your product or service to meet these needs. Finally, you should consider the cost to build, buy or partner to satisfy the gaps in meeting these requirements.

EZ Commerce constructed a simple matrix that yielded dramatic results by clearly communicating information throughout their decision-making process, as depicted in the following chart which extends our earlier example:

Buyer Values	Our Grade	Our Ability to Provide	Customer Benefit
Business Buyers			
Respond to change	1	2	1
Create competitive advantage	2	1	1
Improve channel relationships	2	3	2
Reduce expenses	1	3	1
Adopt easy-to-use products	3	1	2
Increase revenue	2	2	2
Increase vertical competency	2	1	1
IT Buyers			
Comprehensive, integrated	2	2	1
Leverage IT investment	1	3	1
Mission critical	2	2	2
Scalable	1	3	1
Extensible	1	3	1
Reduce deployment complexity	2	2	3

Scale: 1=High, 3=Low

Valuable information can be derived from this simple graphical representation, and subsequent costing exercises can be conducted to determine the real costs, opportunity costs and time frames associated with addressing individual buyer values. Conversely, the relative increases in revenue and customer satisfaction can also be further extrapolated.

As for product development, there are a number of build vs. buy vs. partner models that can be developed to determine which option best suits your business and customer needs. In each case, you should consider the potential benefit, cost and time-to-market differences, and your organization's ability to execute.

Distribution Channel Options

Most channel failures can be traced to undefined strategies that have been described as the "random chance approach," whereby companies continue trying different strategies and tactics until they get it right or go out of business. Conversely, successful alliance and partnership practitioners have intelligently integrated channel activities into their overall corporate operating plans.

So where are the opportunities to align with partners in achieving maximum results—for your company and your customers? Actually, there are numerous prospects for success and failure. The driving principles have to do again with the buyer values and expectations, the channel readiness of your product or solution and your own sales and marketing capabilities.

On the distribution side of the equation, you should begin with an honest assessment of your own channel and product readiness. These initial criteria will help you determine whether your product or solution is channel ready:

- Competitive—It has the right features, functions and benefits.

- Complementary—It enables channel partners to better serve their customers, without introducing additional risk or complexity.
- Complete—It has the right stuff: quality and documentation that is necessary to succeed in the channel.

These simple qualifying criteria also apply when bringing additional products and services into your existing distribution channel.

Channel Agreements

Establishing a multi-channel revenue stream can be a consuming and daunting task for a young enterprise. Especially in the early stages of channel development, it is important to construct smart agreements with the right partners. For instance, value-added reseller agreements should minimally include the following performance criteria:

- Revenue—Each reseller agrees to revenue objectives that qualify them to remain in the program.
- Reporting and communication—Each reseller agrees to publish monthly sales activity reports.

In addition, standard contractual criteria should be included in relevant partner agreements:

- Engagement rules—The protocols that will be followed to maximize revenue and customer satisfaction should be included in the agreement to ensure that channel conflict is minimized.
- Terms—Vendors must agree on price and payment terms, which can vary widely.
- Component or service definition—Agreements need to define components that are being embedded or the services being provided, the characteristics of the resulting offering and which party will provide the integration, project management and design review.
- Training—The agreement should indicate which party is responsible for training sales and internal staff, partners and customers.

- Length—Agreements should establish initial, renewal and termination terms.
- Exclusivity—Most participants would like exclusivity but recognize that it typically applies to only the most powerful vendors.
- Intellectual property—Companies often need to share technology secrets, which puts a premium on protecting intellectual property. Typically, this is resolved through nondisclosure agreements.
- License and component protection—Agreements also need to determine how participants can protect their rights to the component technology when a component supplier buys or merges with a potential competitor.
- Coopetition—Participants should protect themselves against product and service line expansions that compete within each other's respective core market.
- Markets—Some component suppliers are particular about the markets in which their products can be distributed.
- Termination—Agreements should include conditions under which either party can terminate the agreement.
- Product testing—The agreement should define whether the OEM or the supplier will pay to have a component tested.

EZ Commerce Sales Model

EZ Commerce has established a simple selling model that is used by its telemarketing, direct sales and distribution partners. In fact, the company spends a considerable amount of time educating all three parties on the model and requires partners to complete an EZ Commerce workshop before being licensed to sell the EZ Software Series. This also enables EZ Commerce telemarketing professionals to service both direct sales professionals and partners.

The EZ Commerce sales model migrates companies through several prospect identification and qualification phases:

Telemarketing Phases
- Pre-suspect—This category includes the universe of companies that could potentially purchase EZ Commerce products.
- Suspect—They have identified needs that EZ Commerce could resolve.
- Prospect—They are in the target SICs, have specific channel needs that EZ Commerce resolves, are within the target revenue range, have an identified e-commerce project and sponsor, and understand the implementation assessment process.

Direct Sales and Channel Partner Phases
- Qualified Prospect—Companies in this phase have an allocated budget, EZ Commerce understands their decision process and has made the prospect's short list, an estimated close date is known, and a demo/face-to-face meeting is scheduled.
- Implementation Assessment—Prospect agrees to a fee-paid assessment to gather proposal information.
- Proposal—A proposal is delivered to the prospect.
- Client—The new customer is transitioned to the EZ Commerce consulting and client support teams.

Telemarketing has proven to be an important, cost-effective component of the EZ Commerce sales model. Since the complex products require a sophisticated "solution sales" approach, the company has maintained a conservative 1:4 ratio of telemarketers to sales representatives. The specific duties of the telemarketers include:
- Outbound profiling of large accounts;
- Outbound support for regional marketing seminars;
- Inbound support for calls that result from marketing activities; and
- Qualifying companies and opportunities, maintaining productive relationships and migrating them to the qualified prospect phase.

Certainly there are many factors that affect a decision to telemarket, and you should consider whether telemarketing will work for you. The author firmly believes that a smart telemarketing operation can provide high quality, cost-effective lead generation and awareness benefits in business-to-business and business-to-consumer markets. Telemarketing professionals can add significant value when:

- Selling complex, expensive products requires that relationships be established with senior executives who cannot otherwise be reached in an effective and timely manner.
- Selling simple, inexpensive products that do not justify the cost of expensive sales calls.
- Opening new regions or territories that do not yet have direct sales persons or distribution channel partners.
- Generating awareness—quickly—across a targeted list of individuals is a key objective.

In these circumstances, telemarketing can reduce your cost of sale by fifty percent or more and dramatically increase your reach. It is for these reasons that it makes sense to bring telemarketing "in house" whenever possible. If telemarketing is right for you, the sooner you make a commitment to it as a strategic weapon, the faster you will begin to see predictable results.

Be sure to avoid the "ready, fire, aim" pitfall that many high technology organizations fall into. Once you have documented the channel objectives, you should establish programs and policies to govern the relationships and support your partners before you identify, recruit and sign them on. It may seem like common sense, but you would be surprised at the number of times that relationships have been established and revenue goals set, without programs or policies to support them.

Effective channel strategies are essential in today's highly competitive and undifferentiated global marketplace. Leading organizations continue to develop and evolve their competencies to ensure future prosperity and customer satisfaction.

Produce Whole Products

Today, customers are generally more sophisticated and demanding than ever—and rightfully so. The advancement of technology is enabling each of us—and our competitors—to move so quickly and nimbly that customer satisfaction must be met through each of the "whole product" capabilities at our disposal.

According to Theodore Levitt's *The Marketing Imagination*, the whole product model consists of four perceptions of the product that need to be considered and understood:

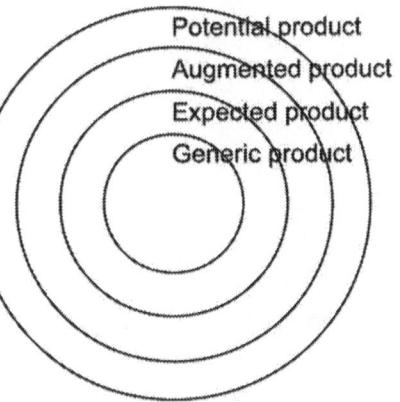

- Generic product—What is actually shipped and written on the sales contract.
- Expected product—What the customer thought they were buying.
- Augmented product—What the product could be with additional product, service and support options.
- Potential product—Finally, what the product could become when its vision is fulfilled and future enhancements are made.

In order for a generic product to become an expected or potential product, shortcomings will need to be addressed. For example, a typical high technology product solution might eventually include the following integrated components to maximize the buyer's experience and satisfaction:

- The base product definition, which should be varied for the needs of a given channel.
- Product packaging considerations that include form vs. function, relative cost vs. desired image, and electronic vs. paper documentation. These issues plus customer expectation are major factors in your packaging strategy.
- Customer and partner education that exceeds the needs of each party.
- User groups and networks that cultivate successful, raving fans.
- Product support and maintenance that results in reference accounts and repeat sales.
- Consulting and integration offerings that dramatically improve customer success ratios.
- Specific partner offerings that may include marketing programs and custom products.
- Standards and procedures that meet customer needs and expectations.
- Additional hardware and software that are needed to optimize product performance.

EZ Commerce Whole Product Platform

After completing a significant number of formal interviews with customers and prospects, and reviewing the results of the competitive analysis from the Marketscape Platform phase, EZ Commerce adopted a whole product model for its e-commerce product.

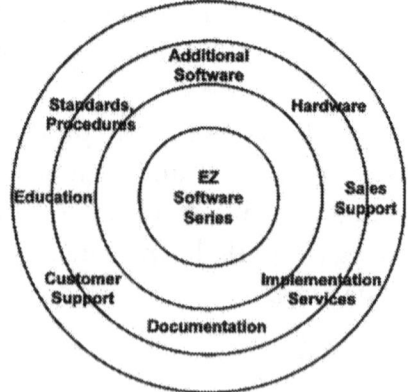

Likewise, the factors that determine the degree of productization that is required for your product are derived from your partner characteristics and customer values. You should spend a considerable amount of time developing your whole product strategy—not only to meet the needs of your customers, but also to save valuable time in developing productive partnerships and alliances.

In this era of sophisticated one-to-one marketing and reference selling, each channel partner and customer must be supported as "a universe of one." Exceeding customer expectation is the minimum requirement, and you will seldom have more than one opportunity to convert a customer into a raving fan. Work smart and do it right the first time.

Finally, the results of your Channel Platform should include channel entry and growth considerations, strategies to identify and secure partners, whole product programs to empower them and policies to govern the rules of engagement throughout your direct and indirect channels.

EZ Commerce Sales Model

EZ Commerce decided to maintain its two-tier sales model whereby senior telemarketing professionals supported an aggressive direct sales force. The company also acknowledged that system integrators—large and small—would be needed to expand into new geographic and vertical markets. Finally, it recognized that its whole product was not yet complete, and that better documentation, packaging and education would be needed to support expansion into alternate distribution channels.

Marketing alliances hold great promise for Performance Marketing professionals who want to achieve leverage and substantial results by sharing expenses, experience and strategies. Of course, Performance Marketing professionals are ultimately accountable for their own results, and knowing what not to pursue can be as rewarding as knowing where to invest resources. Before entering into any channel marketing relationship, be sure the partner is equally motivated before investing precious time toward building a relationship.

Four Cs of Marketing In Action

During the Channel Platform phase, we identify the most effective channels for reaching individual buyers. We also determine how multiple channels will collaborate and interrelate to maximize customer satisfaction while minimizing channel conflict.

Brand Platform

What concerns me is not the way things are,
but rather the way people think they are.
Epictetus, Greek Philosopher

Branding has become a focus of nearly every corporate stakeholder in the new century—perhaps driven by the rapid acceleration in technological innovation which has created a universe of buyers who are never actually known by the seller. Or it could be the speed at which technology is integrated into the products and services themselves, making it nearly impossible for a provider to maintain an edge at all times.

Quality, price, image, and service are all elements of a winning brand. The marketer who builds a brand on price alone will most likely never reach profitable levels of market penetration since loyalty for his product lasts until his competitor offers another year-end discount or holds another fire sale.

When asked to identify the essential elements of a product or solution brand, many marketers will gravitate toward choosing the right name and logo, with little knowledge or understanding of how to:
- Build brand loyalty,
- Create and position the brand,
- Extend the brand with extensions and sub-brands, or
- Add value to the brand through corporate identity and image programs that maximize value.

In order to develop the most valuable, market-crushing brand possible, you will need to reach far beyond the hype and promises made by marketing agencies and instead focus on a few principles. Product brand building is certainly not a new concept; marketing pros in many industries from automobiles to soap and oatmeal were developing leading brands long before Microsoft debuted.

However, the true value of a successful brand has been recognized more recently as Internet and e-commerce implementations and adoption rates have soared. It is in this electronic community environment that brand value takes on renewed meaning. When you don't personally know your buyer and you are a single click away from either a purchase or abandonment, the overall awareness and value of your brand becomes more essential than ever.

Regardless, there are a few basic steps that need to be accomplished before a brand strategy can be developed and implemented:

1. Market and competitive brand perception analysis—A comprehensive review of how competitors are positioning themselves and how their messages resonate with appropriate stakeholders.

2. Internal brand perception analysis—An in-depth review of your own perceptions, objectives and expectations as they pertain to your brand.

3. Stakeholder perception gap analysis—An analytical mapping between the market and internal brand perceptions, and the perceptions and needs of your individual stakeholders.

Once these analyses are complete, you should be in a position to move forward with an intelligent brand development strategy.

EZ Competitive Brand Analysis

After completing these analyses, EZ Commerce prepared a brand/target experience map to study and communicate the business and information technology buyer values that were being addressed by two primary competitors:

Business Buyer Values	Competitor A	Competitor B
• Respond to change	Provides faster time to market and response to change.	Improves time to market.
• Create competitive advantage/ROI		Creates competitive advantage and a higher ROI.
• Improve channel relationships	Allows closer relationships with partners and customers.	
• Reduce expenses		Improves service levels. Reduces operating expenses.
• Adopt easy-to-use products	Is easy to use.	
• Increase revenue	Reduces operating expenses.	
• Increase vertical competency		

Technology Buyer Values	Competitor A	Competitor B
• Comprehensive, integrated	Provides a complete solution.	Offers products based on a common platform.
• Leverage IT investment	Leverages your current IT investment.	Leverages the investment in existing applications.
• Mission critical	Enables mission-critical deployments.	
• Scalable • Extensible	Scales to support high transaction volumes and distributed deployment.	Offers high scalability, reliability and performance. Has an open and extensible architecture.
• Reduce deployment complexity		

And to complete the picture, EZ Commerce prepared similar brand/target experience maps for its own internal brand perception analysis and stakeholder perception gap analysis efforts.

Once this process is complete, which takes significant time and effort to accomplish, you are ready to develop and implement the remaining elements of a winning Brand Platform.

Name, Frame and Claim Your Market

To maximize the value that you realize from a given product or service, you need to name a market segment, frame or define the market and claim dominance within it. Ideally, a winning, high value market segment will be:

- An appealing market that is easy to understand,
- A growing market,
- A large market, and
- A market in which you can dominate.

If your market does not meet these criteria, you may not achieve the valuation that you desire, or enough attention from stakeholders including customers, investors and thought leaders such as industry analyst groups.

Brand Message Hierarchy

While there are many methods for producing an effective message hierarchy, the positioning statement, value proposition and supporting statements should provide an interlocking system of messages and proof points.

The positioning statement reflects the brand essence and serves as the

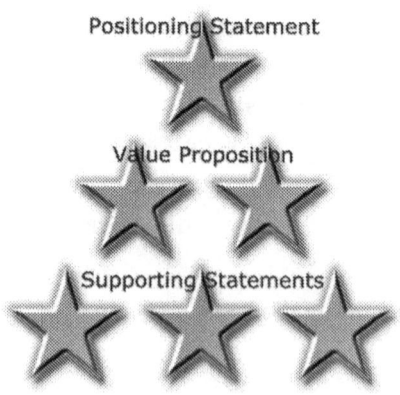

foundation for all communications. The value proposition clearly and powerfully articulates the value that customers receive. And each corresponding supporting statement expresses attributes in ways that resonate with audiences and compel them to action.

Who is the target customer? How does the product cure his pain? Make him successful? Answers to these positioning questions should be simply articulated and supported throughout the message hierarchy.

EZ Commerce Message Hierarchy

EZ Commerce has adopted the following message hierarchy for its Performance Marketing programs:

- Positioning statement—EZ Commerce enables companies to quickly deploy e-commerce solutions that optimize sell-side business processes and information assets that are essential to dominating their markets.
- Value proposition—EZ Commerce products automate business processes and increase the value of information assets that improve business agility, financial performance and brand loyalty across extended enterprise networks.
- Supporting statement I—EZ Software Series deploys rapidly: Out-of-the-box deployment is possible through the open standard-based suite. The rapid e-business deployment methodology improves implementation success and satisfaction. Fixed fee projects and short implementation times result.
- Supporting statement II—EZ Software Series improves business asset performance: Model-based approaches increase agility, competitive advantage and ROI. Self-service application models empower partners, customers and employees by increasing revenues and service levels, and reduce expenses, latency and multi-channel friction by incorporating e-business technology. The series is based on proven, industry best practices and leverages customer investments in existing systems and processes.

- Supporting statement III—EZ Software Series provides end-to-end visibility and control of information and transactions across the extended enterprise. Process and information management support the entire back- to front-office spectrum. The solution integrates and optimizes the three dimensions of e-business: process, information and infrastructure.

Brand Positioning Should Be Maintained

Positioning should always be monitored throughout a product's lifecycle because changes in the competitive landscape and customer demand could alter the overall emphasis or perspective. It should also be noted that a direct relationship exists between the amount of strategic Marketscape Platform research completed and the frequency of change to positioning statements. The more research that is conducted before the Brand Platform development process, the less likely it is that changes are to occur. Hence, another reason to stay focused on buyer values.

Once this message hierarchy has been established, all Communication Platform deliverables and programs should be consistent and supportive—across the organization. This can be especially challenging for dispersed, multinational organizations that are not able to monitor the marketing programs and messages in distant regions. Therefore, special efforts must always be made to maintain the integrity of the message hierarchy.

Constructing the Brand Hierarchy

There are many important considerations that should be made when establishing a brand hierarchy. An effective Brand Platform should include a well-documented brand hierarchy that protects the brand while supporting the organization's expansion into new markets and product lines.

Regardless of the specific situation, the overall recognition of the company name and product name, and the perceived added value of the company name to the product, label or logo should be evaluated. Are these assets that need to be leveraged, or have they not been established in the marketplace? Or they may have negative appeal and should be replaced. And what levels of brand loyalty are associated with the brand? Perhaps the brand enjoys a following of raving fans such as has been established by industry leaders such as Coca-Cola.

Regardless, experienced marketing professionals understand that these assets must be evaluated, and if necessary, research should be conducted to determine their value. Marketing professionals must determine the specific aspects of products and services that are perceived to be superior and inferior.

Market perceptions about the company's strengths and weaknesses should be understood as well as the company's perceived level of competence when solving problems. And how does the competition stack up? What are the competitive strengths and weaknesses? And finally, are there legal or financial issues that are affecting the brand's overall performance?

Companies need to address where to invest and build equity within their brand hierarchy. The rapid proliferation of Internet-based sales and marketing systems has resulted in an increased emphasis on developing corporate umbrella brands that are superior to the product and service line sub-brands. This momentum toward building corporate brands allows sub-brands to be phased out as they lose market prominence—without depreciating overall corporate brand equity.

Four Cs of Marketing In Action

During the Brand Platform phase, we assemble the brand hierarchy that best services our company, customers and distribution channels. Establishing this framework early in the go-to-market process can dramatically reduce rework and expense.

EZ Commerce Brand Hierarchy

Recognizing that its brand is a financial concept which provides distinct financial value to the company, EZ Commerce's brand hierarchy begins at the corporate level, with product- and service-related brand strategies remaining subservient to the corporate brand. It has been architected to maximize value and the overall marketing investment in the brand.

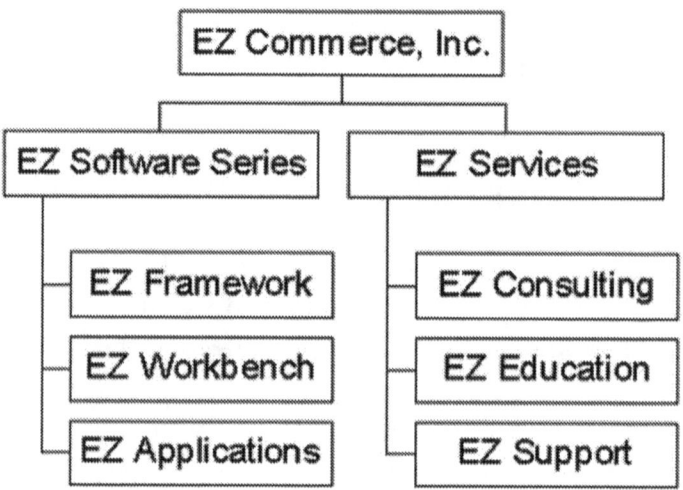

While there are many options for architecting the brand hierarchy, this model has been selected because it leverages the corporate name throughout, it is sufficiently flexible to survive numerous product acquisitions and introductions, and it is relatively inexpensive to maintain.

Leading enterprises such as Oracle and Microsoft have effectively developed and implemented this model of brand hierarchy. In circumstances where there are relatively few products, as in the case of Coca-Cola, it might make sense to create a simple hierarchy in which the company and product brand names are either synonymous or nearly identical.

And occasionally, as in the case of Ty, Inc. and its Beanie Babies, the product brand can become more prominent than the corporate brand which may ultimately result in issues and inefficiencies that must be addressed. For instance, Information Builders' Focus software product was at one time more prominent than the company brand. When Information Builders began to introduce additional products, it did not have a powerful corporate brand to leverage which was unfortunate. In fact, one could argue that the Focus brand equity began to deteriorate as demand for the product waned, leaving the company with neutral and negative brand assets.

Communications Platform

We shall fight them on the beaches. We shall fight on the landing grounds. We shall fight in the fields and in the streets. We shall fight in the hills.
We shall never surrender!
Winston Churchill

Expand and Grow

Now that you have crafted your vision, identified the right segments, buyer values and preferences, established a channel plan and the requirements for the most customer-satisfying whole product, you should be ready to develop a fully-integrated Communications Platform. To maximize your marketing return on investment and overall company value, you will need to combine traditional marketing programs and methods with newer sales and marketing technologies.

Successful strategic marketing is about brains, not brawn. Shotgun sportsmen have fallen prey to sophisticated sharpshooters who understand that information, and how it is used, is what separates mass marketers from strategic, technology-enabled Performance Marketing professionals.

Information is the key. Identifying segments. Conquering them one at a time and reference selling. The alternative is a dry river bed where "could haves, would haves, and should haves" once flowed freely.

Technology-Enabled Sales and Marketing

Whether you are promoting financial services or high technology products, developing data base marketing or data warehousing systems, executing cross selling programs or implementing maintenance programs you will need sophisticated technology-enabled sales and marketing capabilities. And do not wait until you desperately need them. It can take a significant amount of time to establish the infrastructure to engage in this level of technological marketing warfare.

If you haven't developed an inventory of strategic and tactical technologies that are available to empower your business, this is the time to do so—but don't go it alone. Get some expert advice. Missteps in execution can cost you dearly in the Internet age, when entire programs are launched—from early concept through execution and measurement—in a few short months.

And don't abandon your buyers—or your instincts—as you lean toward execution. Continue to focus on the values that stakeholder customers and prospects, editors and analysts hold dearly. A few additional comments about your marketing mix:

- In the advertising world, winning campaigns align with buyer values and behaviors. Losing campaigns can still win Clio awards for your agency, but not for you.
- Through effective public relations programs, awareness and recognition are earned, not given. You must recognize the essential roles that analyst, press, and investor relations play in your business, and the significant time and effort that is required to educate and develop valuable relationships.
- Web site development and redevelopment services can help you demonstrate your creative prowess, but that is only the beginning. The Internet must be completely integrated throughout the entire Communications Platform, and technologies such as content management should help drive your messages through multiple media—paper, electronic and film.

- Event and trade show marketing must be fully integrated. When executed properly, event marketing can generate sales leads, increase brand awareness and employee recruiting opportunities, and support valuable market and competitive research efforts.
- Smart direct marketing in this era should be synonymous with "one-to-one" database marketing. This equates to good business and pure profit.

And the list goes on to include areas such as distribution policies, pricing analysis and modeling, and customer reference programs. These are all areas in which you will need sufficient traditional and technology-based proficiency.

Properly aligning your marketing programs and sales model can bring your direct and indirect channels to new levels. But to ensure that marketing programs are aligned with strategic corporate initiatives, marketing executives should be compensated for achieving revenue objectives—and punished when they are not met.

EZ Commerce Market Expansion Strategies

To support the strategies that were previously established in the Marketscape and Channel Platform phases, the EZ Commerce marketing department has chosen to implement a viral, dialogue-based marketing program that engages customers and prospects on a frequent basis. The approach combines fundamental, baseline programs with vertical go-to-market strategies.

To support these strategies, EZ Commerce intends to leverage its best customers to achieve market penetration. When evaluating its brand assets, the company determined that its blue chip customer base was largely comprised of raving fans that were supportive of the company and could be counted on to help EZ Commerce succeed.

The company's viral go-to-market strategy leverages blue chip refer-ences in three primary ways—by marketing to:
- New divisions within an organization,
- Associated businesses (e.g., suppliers) within the same or similar vertical market, and
- Competitive organizations within a vertical.

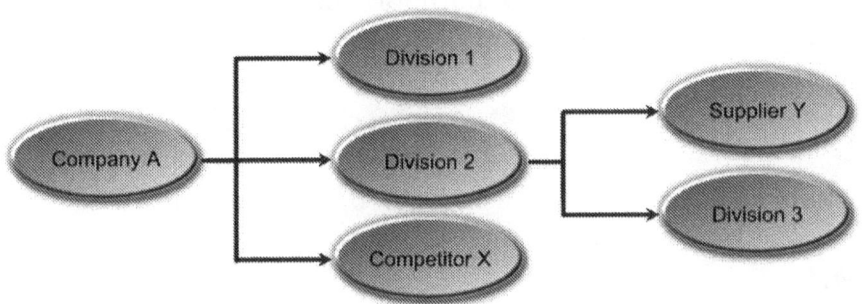

The company further decided that it could efficiently increase brand recognition and revenue through strategic partnerships and programs. EZ Commerce recognizes that this may require private labeling or bundling strategies that are not currently in place.

And based on input from EZ Commerce's sales organization, the company determined that it could raise sales transaction amounts by focusing on high profile ROI- and business case-oriented programs that promote the success that customers have had with the EZ Software Series. These include special reference programs to nurture its relation-ship with key customers.

Finally, given the importance of expanding into global market seg-ments, EZ Commerce was determined to leverage its high profile pro-grams and successes with multinational customers as beachheads in Asia and Europe.

EZ Commerce Brand Development

Branding is perhaps the most important marketing element for EZ Commerce's ongoing success and growth. Remaining customer-focused, brand development strategies are orchestrated around customer needs rather than EZ Commerce-created differentiation. As such, EZ Commerce recognizes three distinct responsibilities—improving employee morale, client acquisition and client retention—for its branding strategy. All branding programs are initiated with these in mind.

To build brand quickly, EZ Commerce continues to develop and leverage its:

- Blue chip customer relationships through media relations, speaking engagements, analyst relations, testimonial advertising, case studies, etc.
- Partners and alliances through co-marketing opportunities such as event marketing.
- Employees through speaking engagements, article placements, etc.
- Software and technology by promoting the benefits that can be derived from EZ Commerce solutions.
- Processes and methods that result in repeatable high quality implementations.

Marketing Production Schedule

As such, EZ Commerce developed an integrated marketing production schedule that it uses to manage and communicate its marketing activities by calendar month within the following categories:

- Event Marketing—Conferences, tradeshows and seminars, speaking opportunities, and employee and board meetings.
- Communications—Direct marketing, Web and interactive marketing, and advertising.

- Public Relations—Media, industry analyst, customer, community, and investor relations.
- Product Marketing—Sales and corporate presentations, product launch management and strategic Performance Marketing activities.
- Sales Programs—From brochures to customer visit and customer reference programs.

Product Launch Considerations

This time, like all times, is a very good one,
if we but know what to do with it.
Ralph Waldo Emerson

You've prepared for countless weeks and months. Painstakingly swept through every last detail. The hour is upon you. Each and every eye is watching. And you are totally prepared because you have a proven product launch framework that won't let you down. Or do you?

Introducing a new product into the market can be the most exhilarating experience a marketing professional—and an entire organization—will experience. It is the culmination of untold effort and creativity across the entire company. And the stakes couldn't be higher.

Whatever you do, be sure that it is done with intensity. In an era when major corporations move from idea to launch in 4-5 months, soft launches are out of the question. These trials cause disconnects between technology, strategy and marketing communications, and can have disastrous effects resulting from expensive missed opportunities.

A scalable and extensible cross-organizational product launch framework can make all the difference in ensuring that you achieve maximum results from your efforts. The author has used a common methodology for a range of global product launches including e-business, telecommunication and ERP software. The results can be tremendous—a carefully planned product launch will build brand value and get the all important "buzz" going for your offering, resulting in a dominant market position.

Getting Started

A successful product launch framework includes a repeatable launch process, an integrated set of functions that are performed by different departments, all-important executive commitment and ownership for the process, and a coordinated product launch plan. These elements must be supported by a documented approval process, a committed budget, and clear product segmentation and positioning statements.

An initial step in developing a product launch plan is to assemble a cross functional team (CFT) that will be responsible for coordinating and contributing toward a successful launch. Each individual member should have assigned responsibilities for meeting product launch objectives. These responsibilities can be described as a set of parallel activities that support the successful product positioning and launch.

It is also important that one individual be clearly assigned and empowered with the responsibility of managing the overall product launch process. This owner should be responsible for:

- Managing the overall product launch,
- Hosting the CFT meetings,
- Maintaining the project schedule, and
- Reporting progress and escalating issues for resolution.

For the purposes of our case study, the EZ Commerce CFT has prepared the following objectives and responsibilities for each of its functions:

Overall Functional Responsibilities

- Participate in the Cross Functional Team.
- Ensure that all employees understand and participate in this important program and event.

Marketing Responsibilities

- Develop and oversee overall launch plans.
- Develop the product positioning and supporting case studies.
- Develop and execute marketing communications plans that demonstrate industry leadership.
- Update and maintain the brand hierarchy.

Sales Responsibilities

- Develop the appropriate sales/distribution models.
- Support beta program recruitment and manage customer relationships.
- Train and enable sales persons to support and promote the new product.

Partner Responsibilities

- Ensure that partners are trained and enabled.

Consulting Responsibilities

- Define the appropriate consulting models.
- Train and enable consultants to support product implementations.
- Develop customer reference sites.

Development Responsibilities

- Deliver a defect-free product.
- Ensure that the whole product is complete.
- Ensure that the Cross Functional Team is aware of product delivery status at all times.

Finance and Operations Responsibilities

- Develop financial models (e.g., profitability, order forecasts, etc.)
- Develop/amend legal agreements and documentation.
- Develop relevant operational models.

So exactly who are the audiences for the product launch process? Certainly there are many different constituencies, but communication efforts should be concentrated and customized for all primary company stakeholders, regardless of geographic location. The following objectives should be considered for each stakeholder group:

- Customers—Instilling confidence that they made the right decision to select your product or service. For technology products, ensuring that upgrade and migration processes are painless.
- Prospects—Instilling confidence that your product has been developed with their very requirements in mind.
- Employees—Orienting each employee toward "quality" as they contribute toward the release, celebrating the combined effort, and educating each employee on the product and positioning.
- Partners—Instilling confidence that they have invested their precious time and resources with the right partner—you! And ensuring that they have been fully integrated into the launch process—especially non-domestic partners.
- Investors—Renewing your vision and demonstrating your down payment toward greater future earnings from their investments.
- Community members—Celebrating the progress and culture that you have established, along with the contribution of talent and treasure that you have shared—your company is the place to be!
- Key influencers—Communicating your vision and educating industry and financial analysts who can serve as advisors and references.

Product Launch Process

Clear product or service positioning is critical to the success of any launch. If positioning has not been clearly defined, refer back to the Brand Platform section of this book to refine your positioning statement, value proposition and supporting statements.

The product's early adoption or beta program is another important aspect of the launch process. These programs are required to:

- Cultivate a number of key customers who have enough success with the product to serve as sources for case studies and references for prospects, editors and industry analysts.
- Entice the distribution channel(s) with enough excitement to convince them to invest their resources with the new product or release.
- Ensure that product quality—defect-free and feature-rich—is satisfactory.

The international marketplace has explicit requirements that demand attention during the product launch process. For instance, specific product requirements, beta program participation, and pricing and legal considerations should be addressed:

- Product requirements—If the product needs to be localized, then you must ensure that it is architected properly. Localization includes many aspects from interfacing to other vendor products to translating data formats, currencies, screens, documentation, messages and help files.
- Beta program participation—Non-domestic sites should be included in beta programs for the very same reasons that domestic customers are included. We live in a global economy—plan ahead and seize the day.
- Price considerations—Ensure that special pricing programs and incentives can be customized for local markets.
- Legal considerations—Agreements and amendments should be worded with the international community in mind.

Recognizing the positive impact that a formal launch program can have, EZ Commerce has prepared a detailed product launch checklist that integrates activities throughout its organization. The complete checklist which is provided in the appendix, includes the following categories:

- Product launch operations
- Whole product creation
- Beta process
- Pricing and finance
- Public Relations
- Communications
- Sales, channel and services enablement
- International
- Training
- Order fulfillment
- Manufacturing/packaging
- Distribution
- Follow-up and evaluation

Code to Commerce is not simply about traditional marketing communications, but it instead attempts to position marketing communications on a more strategic plane within the Performance Marketing Lifecycle. Too often, marketing professionals are driven to the end game only to arrive without the required tools to win and sustain competitive advantage.

Four Cs of Marketing In Action

During the Communication Platform phase, we identify the programs that will most effectively meet the needs of our stakeholders—including the company, customer and channel.

Technology Platform

No problem can be solved within
the same consciousness which caused it.
Albert Einstein

The digital age is exploding, and Performance Marketing professionals are leading the revolution to capitalize on and shape it by implementing technology-enabled sales and marketing solutions at an unprecedented pace.

Each phone call, product purchase, financial transaction and electronic tollbooth crossing has the potential of registering meaningful consumer information. And now that satellites are capable of tracking our every movement, whether by automobile or on foot with a cellular phone, life will never be the same.

As a result of this influx of valuable customer data and the sufficient maturity of technology-enabled sales and marketing (TESM) solutions to support Mainstreet America, customer churn, personalized, one-to-one customer interaction and sales force efficiency have become boardroom topics in many industries.

Technology-Enabled Sales and Marketing

TESM is an enterprise business strategy that actually precedes the identification and selection of solutions that typically include software, hardware and service vendors. While specific goals of a TESM implementation will vary, there are marketing-specific metrics, derived from information in the Marketscape Platform chapter, that should be thoroughly understood before software and hardware solutions are evaluated and purchased.

Customer profitability is a key metric for Performance Marketing professionals that should be known prior to choosing a specific solution. Are 20 percent of the customers generating 80 percent of the revenue? Which customers are requiring the most support? And what are the trends with respect to customer profitability?

By analyzing and trending customer profitability, you will be able to determine which groups of customers are growing and which are declining in number. Perhaps most importantly, with additional analysis you should be able to determine *why* customers are in certain groups. And once you have determined this, you are in a position to agree upon specific objectives for your TESM initiatives.

A second key metric is *customer attrition*. Extending the duration of existing customer relationships is vital to the health of any organization—especially in the digital age when many companies maintain virtual and relatively precarious relationships with their customers. Metrics should therefore be in place to monitor the number and percentage of customers that are in given categories over time.

Is this percentage increasing, decreasing or remaining relatively constant? Specifically, which customers are leaving and what is causing them to break ranks? Are channel partners becoming more focused on price or quality? What about the end customer? Of those that are leaving, were they profitable or unprofitable customers? And where on Earth are they going?

Customer retention programs may be an important outcome of your TESM initiative, but you will need to collect and analyze customer attrition data before making intelligent determinations.

Lifetime value analysis is a third metric that should be completed. By understanding the value of individuals and specific groups of customers, you are able to initiate programs that alter customer behavior and improve the profitability of those relationships. Marketing programs that increase your share of wallet by cross- and up-selling additional products to a given customer or household are natural opportunities.

Analyzing customer satisfaction, needs and preferences is an important phase that should be completed before a specific TESM solution is implemented. Once customers are formally surveyed, the information can be used to initiate marketing programs that are designed to improve customer satisfaction. This information is also invaluable for attracting and retaining new customers, and determining features for new product and support offerings.

Additional benefits include lower sales and marketing costs, and better customer service. When you are in a position to better understand your customers and their specific needs, you will be able to implement programs that realize greater economies of scale while remaining highly personalized. Not all customers will be treated the same, but you will be in a better position to direct your precious time and people resources and avoid opportunity costs.

To fully capitalize on the rich influx of marketing data, companies in virtually every industry invest in TESM systems. As previously discussed, there are many business reasons for this. The following contain more exhaustive details that should be used to evaluate your TESM objectives and ultimate payback:

Technology-Enabled Sales Objectives
- Reduce sales cycle times by handling sales objectives quickly.
- Reduce order errors by configuring valid orders.
- Increase customer satisfaction by configuring solutions correctly.
- Increase customer retention and renewal rates.
- Increase revenue per order by up selling and cross selling.
- Increase new product revenue.

- Increase selling knowledge by utilizing just-in-time training while reducing the cost to train a sales person.
- Reduce forecast preparation by enabling sales pipeline roll-ups.
- Increase global account sales by gaining visibility into major account activity and aligning distributed sales teams.
- Increase sales person productivity.
- Increase Web sales by personalizing Web buying.
- Increase gross margin per order by measuring order margins.
- Increase planning capabilities by creating and realigning sales territories.
- Increase the effectiveness and capabilities of sales management.

Technology-Enabled Marketing Objectives

- Increase marketing campaign efficiency and effectiveness.
- Reduce marketing campaign cycle times.
- Reduce marketing overhead.
- Increase cash flow by better utilizing marketing funds.
- Increase market share by measuring share growth/loss for product, division or company segments.
- Increase sales productivity by incenting selling behavior.
- Increase the company's ability to support a multiple-channel sales structure.
- Increase the overall performance of marketing management.

So where is the payback? Industry executives continue to cite improving services for customers, reducing costs and increasing profits as being among their top business objectives. Consequently, corporate investment in technology-enabled sales and marketing solutions continues to increase as more business leaders view marketing as a strategic investment, rather than an expense.

By now it should be obvious that you will need to conduct a realistic assessment of your objectives and gain a thorough understanding of your customers—their behaviors, values and requirements. The result is that you will be in a better position to align your business and marketing strategies with their expectations, manage customer information as a valuable asset, measure customer value and monitor attrition.

Once you have integrated information throughout the business, especially from various business units and geographies that have different points of contact with customers and markets, you will be able to increase your brand-building capability and improve your ability to affect profitability and the overall customer experience.

TESM Landscape

While marketing's predominant focus is often on the marketing-specific elements of TESM, Performance Marketing professionals should have a general understanding of the various solutions that comprise the vast TESM landscape.

Broadly speaking, TESM enables businesses to market to, sell to and support customers—ideally for a lifetime. Fortunately, the solutions for accomplishing these activities have become tightly coupled and integrated from the back office database to the front office user interface and multiple customer touch points.

The adjacent diagram portrays the many TESM solutions that can be leveraged during the life of a customer relationship. Performance Marketing professionals should have knowledge of these technologies, and how they service the customer and impact the overall business. Several of the more common sales and marketing system categories are noted below:

- Sales Force Automation systems include contact and opportunity management capabilities, and enable team selling across direct, inside sales, partner and executive ranks.

- Product Configurators enable sales professionals, partners and customers to configure and price product offerings.
- Self-service systems empower sales professionals, partners and customers to order products and access restricted material via the Internet, intranet or extranet.
- Content Management applications allow enterprises to view and access text, graphics animation and video content in a secure and authorized environment.
- Call Management systems are used to auto-dial outgoing and log incoming telephone calls, and manage the transaction from initiation through closure.
- Field Service systems include applications for call management and routing, and workforce scheduling and dispatching.
- Personalization technologies create and adjust user profiles to match content to individual interests, buying patterns or specified permissions.
- Analytic systems support strategic decision-making processes by providing software for ad hoc querying, reporting and analysis.
- Marketing Automation systems allow marketing professionals and sales organizations to implement multi-channel campaigns and track the results.

Marketing professionals will need to work closely and strategically with their information technology counterparts to ensure that TESM systems are planned and implemented to support the organization's most strategic business objectives.

Evaluate the Options

Evaluating and selecting a service provider is considered by many to be more important than choosing the actual software and hardware. And over time, you should expect service-related costs to far outweigh the expenses involved with other elements of the overall TESM solution. Therefore, when evaluating service providers, be sure that they have:

- Strategic and tactical sales and marketing best practices and process expertise within the given industry vertical.
- Business transformation and change management expertise that includes relevant project management experience.
- Post-implementation support capabilities—in many respects, the work only begins when the system is complete.

Selecting the actual software can be an equally daunting task. While your service provider can assist in this process, you should never divorce yourself from the process. Should relations falter between you and your service provider, you don't want to be left with an expensive, complex infrastructure that cannot be easily implemented or supported by another party.

A TESM software selection should also be compatible with your existing technology infrastructure or platform. And the overall selection should be capable of supporting sales, marketing, and customer service across the entire enterprise without requiring that data be fragmented or duplicated. A company should be able to incrementally add new functionality, and the solution should scale with larger volumes of data, additional employees, new products in the portfolio, etc. Finally, the solution should support the latest standards that are in place at the time of purchase.

This is not to say that a single software vendor will satisfy all of your needs. Quite the contrary. As you move from sales to marketing to customer service, you may find that a dozen or more best-of-breed products are required to comprise the total solution. But these products must work together and support common standards, have simple interfaces, share corporate data and business rules, and be easily customized.

TESM solutions are sufficiently mature today to warrant such demands. High quality solutions that can be cleanly and cost-effectively implemented are available to companies large and small, assuming that the implementation services provider performs as expected.

Consider the Costs

Certainly, not sponsoring a serious TESM initiative can have disastrous effects on your business—especially when your competitors are already intensely engaged in understanding their customers. Remaining idle can result in missed opportunities from which you cannot recover, given the time and expense that it takes to win a new customer and the importance of maintaining a stellar brand image when alternative products are a simple click away.

Referring to the Channel Platform discussion of whole product components, you should expect to find that the software itself represents approximately 25-30 percent of overall CRM project costs. Other costs include implementation and training services, hardware and telecommunications which are often overlooked.

Four Cs of Marketing In Action

During the Technology Platform phase, we analyze the potential for the strategic use of technology throughout the sales and marketing mix. Special emphasis is placed on efficient collaboration capabilities that can result across our company, channel and customer environments.

TESM at EZ Commerce

EZ Commerce determined that the most important decision that it could make was to simply get started! It established goals, assembled a cross-functional team and developed a simple plan to address its most pressing issues and greatest opportunities.

Since it is an emerging company with a relatively small customer base, it determined that investing in a technology-enabled *sales* solution would meet its most strategic objectives of opening new markets where it did not have a presence and generating more qualified leads for its direct sales force.

In establishing requirements for its TESM solution—comprised of services, software and hardware—it determined that a scalable solution that would enable it to easily add marketing and customer service capabilities would be of significant benefit and would carry it forward for many years and customers to come.

The company's cross-functional team which was led by a technology marketing consultant, recommended that it begin with a telemarketing program that was supported by sales force automation and customer contact management technology. The program had the following objectives to:

- Generate leads in existing and new territories.
- Increase revenue by providing more qualified leads that would improve sales force productivity and raise average transaction values.
- Create a strong, high value brand by introducing EZ Commerce to and establishing relationships with key decision-makers in designated target markets.
- Create awareness for its market category among these same target markets.

To accomplish these objectives, the EZ Commerce TESM-enabled telemarketing program provided:

- Outbound call support—Following up on seminars, maintaining conversations and relationships with prospects, and cold calling from lists.
- Inbound call support—Responding to inquiries that have been generated through other marketing programs.
- Sales support—Profiling prospects and transitioning qualified leads.

After several months, the program began to pay substantial dividends. EZ Commerce was able to add new customers and open offices in new regions. A significant additional benefit was that its sales people became more productive since they were being supported by a team of dedicated telemarketing professionals.

Measure and Evaluate

Information has to be organized
so it questions and challenges
a company's strategy.
Peter Drucker

Accountability. More than ever before, marketing organizations are being held accountable for their contribution to the wealth of the overall organization. As a result of being recognized for the financial importance that a brand can have on an organization's health, marketing measurement has been elevated to the most senior executive and strategic boardroom levels. Marketing is now equally under fire for what they spend, the opportunities they seize—or squander—and the results they deliver.

But the story grows even more complex as marketing functions and campaigns become dispersed throughout distributed organizations of all sizes and industries—from high technology startups to leading multinationals. Addressing the increasing requirements to generate and measure results, Performance Marketing professionals look to integrate technology-enabled sales and marketing across their entire organizations—bridging research and development, product management, product marketing, marketing communications, sales and channels, customer support, finance and operations—to help them achieve their objectives.

Establishing effective marketing measurement programs is becoming increasingly important—to marketers themselves—as they are asked to measure tangible and intangible factors. Revisiting our earlier discussion, Performance Marketing professionals focus simultaneously on three important areas of the revenue model: acquiring new customers, extending the duration of customer relationships and enhancing the profitability of existing customers.

While executive management has become increasingly focused on bottom line cost reductions, recent trends indicate that they are now focusing on the top line opportunities such as sell-side e-commerce across distributed partner networks. To the marketing professional, this means they too must be in a position to contribute toward both of these measures within their overall organization. They must learn to do more with less—and they will be measured on both.

Balanced marketing scorecards can help manage key business indicators across the organization and can be used to educate management on the value that marketing brings to an organization. If marketing is to be distributed throughout a large, multinational organization, then the corporate office should be responsible—and measured—for its ability to build and manage brand standards and reusable marketing components that can be localized internationally with consistency. Accordingly, regional Performance Marketing professionals should be held accountable for their ability to enforce those same brand standards in their spheres of control.

Executive Communication

As with other professions and disciplines, Performance Marketing executives become masters at core competencies that are directly related to disciplined marketing management:

- Communicating with executive management—Peer executives must "buy into" and fully understand marketing strategies and measurements. Because marketing and branding are the responsibility of

each and every corporate citizen, marketing executives must be constant advocates for their initiatives.
- Demonstrating fiscal responsibility—Performance Marketing executives are masters at understanding how their function integrates throughout the entire enterprise. Marketing executives must therefore possess general business and finance skills, and should operate within an agreed upon budget.
- Creating reusable strategies and tactics—Ethnocentrism is a cardinal sin for the Performance Marketing executive. Each and every message, brochure, program and strategy must be created with global markets and marketing organizations in mind. This results in consistent branding and extremely cost effective operations.

Marketing Compensation

So exactly how should the Performance Marketing executive be compensated? If there is not significant "leverage" which is based on revenue and profitability, then there will never be enough peer executive buy in, nor will the marketing executive be properly motivated. In order to achieve the desired results, approximately 25-40 percent of a marketing executive's compensation should be based on revenue and profitability.

So how do you keep score? Organizations must establish efficient, equitable measurement and evaluation programs early in the project planning stages. Marketing audits can then be performed to determine the return on investment and the value that has been increased.

EZ Commerce Marketing Measurement

Integrated with its technology-enabled sales and marketing solution, EZ Commerce invested in an analytical application that enables its product marketing analysts to measure "key business indicators" that were agreed-to by executive management. These performance criteria are categorized and listed below:

Performance Criteria

- Total new accounts, net additions and lost accounts.
- Revenue by product, channel, customer segment (demographic, socioeconomic, psychographic, descriptive or behavioral).
- Total leads generated and total leads by campaign.
- Leads by control group and offer.
- Cost per lead.

Ranking Criteria

- Revenue by customer (80/20 rule).
- Lifetime value of a customer.
- Revenue by product, market segment, SIC segment, sales representative.

Trending Criteria

- Revenue by product, channel, customer segment, market segment, SIC segment, sales representative.
- Sales volume by product, market segment, SIC segment.
- Profit by product, market segment, SIC segment, sales representative.
- Market growth by segment, SIC segment.
- Inventory churn by season, geography, quarter.

Comparison Criteria

- Market share (percent of market penetration).
- Sales volume variance (MTD, YTD).
- Profit variance (MTD, YTD).
- Revenue variance (MTD, YTD).
- External information comparisons (benchmarks).
- Market basket analysis and cross-selling analyses.
- Leads by control group and offer.

Reports Criteria

- Standard profit and loss, and financial reports.
- Standard sales reports, exception reports and custom reports.

EZ Commerce was committed to implementing its system early in the company's lifecycle. As a result, it was able to implement a baseline system quickly and grow it incrementally.

Internet Marketing Metrics

Finally, a note regarding Internet marketing metrics. Given the interest in this evolving area of measurement, there are several metrics that should be considered:

- Reach—The percentage of the target audience that you are able to touch.
- Engage—The percentage that you are actually able to keep in a healthy conversation.
- Conversion—The customers that buy, sign up for a seminar, sign up for a newsletter, or take another desired action.
- Abandonment—It happens more than we care to admit. Find out why!
- Retention—Reward customers for coming back. It's less expensive than acquiring a new customer.

Every Performance Marketing executive, regardless of company size, should be integrating technology for competitive advantage—throughout each phase of the sales and marketing lifecycle.

Organizing for Success

Moving your product from code to commerce is an intense, architected process that requires committed people who are armed with advanced skills and methods. As such, there are many factors that you should consider when building a world-class marketing organization.

Generally speaking, marketing functions are often categorized as product marketing, product management and marketing communications. Of course there are many adaptations of this which could include functions such as telemarketing, brand management, sales enablement and business development.

Product marketing is perhaps the most important—and least understood—marketing function. Successful product marketing organizations are staffed with senior professionals who demonstrate a unique blend of technology, marketing and general business skills. In a single day, they may find themselves going toe-to-toe with technologists, presenting to prospects or customers, and preparing a product release plan. These are the Performance Marketing professionals who:

- Develop business and product strategies.
- Conduct competitive research and produce analysis briefs.
- Develop and articulate marketing messages at category and product levels.
- Produce content for marketing collateral and sales presentations.
- Produce sales enablement materials and programs.
- Publish sales and marketing analysis reports.
- Conduct market research and produce business cases for new initiatives.

- Identify and publish whole product needs.
- Develop and publish pricing models.
- Establish and maintain positive relationships with showcase reference clients.
- Participate in product beta programs to establish early references.

Product management professionals, conversely, are often described as development-facing. While they must be in complete touch with customers and the market, they often primarily serve the research and development organization. This important function typically:
- Prepares product requirements and specifications.
- Prioritizes product enhancements.
- Defines and produces product packaging.
- Manages product beta programs.

Marketing communications and public relations are the most common marketing functions. This includes a wide array of activities and programs from public relations to advertising and direct, event and Internet marketing.

EZ Commerce Marketing

And then there are the permutations. For instance, EZ Commerce decided to include telemarketing within its global marketing organization. After much discussion with the sales organization, it was decided that telemarketing should be closely aligned with strategic marketing programs—and leveraged and integrated wherever possible. Public relations reports directly to the head of marketing, with at dotted line relationship to the CFO. This is due in part to the important emphasis being placed on the investor relations.

However you decide to organize and evolve your marketing organization, you need to be forward-looking and build flexibility into the model. Hire smart people, anticipate change and rely on a proven marketing methodology.

It is the surest bet for making it from *Code to Commerce*.

Appendix

Lucky Software Case Study

Lucky Software is a fictional emerging company that is poised to take on established players in key markets. Its founder named the company after preparing his initial business plan, stating that "they would need a lot of luck to co-exist with Macrosoft," but added that with the right management team, market timing and execution, they could indeed accomplish their objectives.

The Internet-based business intelligence market segment (e.g., report writing software) was chosen for this case study because it is familiar to most readers—regardless of industry.

Finally, every effort has been made to streamline this case study for maximum benefit and relevance to the reader. While it is therefore a subset of a complete Performance Marketing Platform, the practical application of concepts is actually more comprehensive at times than the previous *Code to Commerce* chapters.

The author hopes that you find it useful.

Introduction

Based on initial guidance, Excelsis Group has worked diligently with Lucky Software to develop this Performance Marketing Platform, which serves as the foundation upon which to launch Lucky's go-to-market strategy.

Situation Analysis

Lucky has a significant opportunity to influence and capture a share of the broad and growing Internet-based business intelligence market category. In evidence of this, Lucky has:
- Developed substantial expertise in the business intelligence sector;
- Produced unique and robust business intelligence applications; and
- Generated significant interest among investors and an encouraging number of customers and prospects.

While Lucky understands its solution to be fairly unique, it recognizes that appropriate market timing is essential to achieving investor goals and objectives. As such, Lucky is approaching an important milestone in its evolution as it transitions toward becoming a commercialized software solution provider. This transition is expected to bring new opportunities—along with greater challenges and expectations.

Objectives

To date, Lucky has invested extensively in research and development, and to a lesser extent in sales and marketing. As a result, Lucky is now increasing its focus on near-term marketing objectives, which will enable the business to:
- Generate a significant increase in revenue; and
- Generate valuable awareness as a serious player and industry thought leader.

Strategies

Working with Excelsis Group, the strategies that the Lucky marketing organization will use to realize these objectives include:
- Develop a competitive marketing platform from which to conduct business;

- Execute the resulting go-to-market strategy and integrated marketing plan; and
- Launch Lucky and its products to the global marketplace.

These strategies will enable Lucky to generate the credibility and platform that is necessary for successful business outcomes.

Executive Summary

Excelsis Group has developed this Performance Marketing Platform to meet the essential needs of Lucky leadership across major company disciplines.

Business and Financial Executives

For the company's business and financial executives, this plan provides:

- Baseline information for understanding a complex, competitive market landscape.
- Input to formulating the financial requirements that lie ahead—and where to allocate funds.
- A basis for understanding the convergence of market segments and solutions that is currently underway.

Marketing Organization

For the marketing organization, this plan provides:

- Baseline information for completion of the Performance Marketing Platform.
- Input to determine a winning go-to-market strategy.
- Strategic and tactical input for developing integrated marketing plans.
- Input to the global expansion and product launch plans.

Sales and Channel Organizations

For the sales and channel professional, this plan provides:
- Strategic and tactical input for partner programs, partner selection and acquisition plans, and vertical industry selection.
- High-level competitive intelligence for the sales organization.
- Input to validate the current pricing models.

Research and Development

For research and development, this plan provides:
- Input to understanding the technology and standards that are leading in the marketplace.
- Strategic and tactical input to elements that comprise leading whole products.
- Input to understanding the mature levels of productization that exist in this market.
- Input to short- and medium-term product plans.

Performance Marketing Platform

The agreed approach for Excelsis Group and Lucky Software to achieve these objectives centers on the development of Marketscape, Channel, Brand, Communications and Technology Platforms within the overall Performance Marketing Platform.

The approach begins with a clear understanding of Lucky's strategic vision, market opportunity, product benefits and competitive challenges. Buyer segment profiles are then developed—including the specific challenges that customers and prospects face. From there, detailed strategic marketing plans are developed and implemented. And throughout the entire process, we look for opportunities to integrate and leverage a technology platform that will enable you to exceed your business objectives for years to come.

Marketscape Platform

Services

Conduct research to develop an overview of competitive and related offerings, along with market opportunities. A fully developed Marketscape Platform provides keen insight as to the best possible means of taking your product or service to market and increasing your brand equity.

Deliverables

- Assessment of Lucky's core competencies.
- Analysis of key competitors.
- Competitive market segments based on industry served, the corresponding product offering functionality and buyer profiles (e.g., values and requirements).
- Market opportunity analysis including identification of key constituents and stakeholders.

Lucky's Vision

Lucky has adopted a simple and forward-looking vision statement for its business:

> *Lucky's vision is to ensure that information assets*
> *are accessible from anywhere on the planet.*

Market Demands

The demands of globalization and increased worker mobility open significant opportunities for Lucky. According to a leading industry analyst group, the total U.S. mobile and remote worker population is expected to increase 40% in the next four years to nearly 60 million. This population includes:

- Telecommuters who work at home for an employer three days or more per month,

- Mobile professionals who travel away from their office at least 20% of the time,
- Mobile data collectors who are typically field service people, and
- Work extenders who are employees that need irregular access to their office from remote locations for 20% of the standard workweek.

During the same period, enterprises face significant challenges to true virtual access, due to the following roadblocks:
- Mixed application environments make it difficult to deploy the full digital workplace to all users,
- Mixed device environments are increasingly popular and are causing accessibility and support problems,
- Remote user explosion has proliferated the diversity of network connection types and protocols,
- Extended enterprise demands for suppliers, distributors and customers create application deployment issues including performance and security,
- Security continues to be a boardroom issue due to the amount of sensitive business information that is being proliferated across the globe.

Software Operating Environments

On the client, a combination of Windows versions will dominate the desktop multipurpose computer. While the Mac and Linux client will have shares around 5%, these shares are not growing fast enough to attract any but niche software plays.

On the server, three operating environments—Unix, Linux and Windows—will contend for the Internet initiative workloads. Of these, Windows will have the largest share, but analysts expect Linux to have the fastest-growing share, increasing to nearly 40% by the end of the forecast period.

The combined growth of Linux and the continuing dominance of Windows on the server platforms represent a significant opportunity for Lucky. This also presents an opportunity for Lucky to garner a following of early adopter software developers.

Initial Target Segments

Based on the above vision and market information, Excelsis Group recommends that Lucky consider the following segments in its go-to-market strategy:

- Enterprise—Capital Goods
- Enterprise—Distribution
- Enterprise—Financial Services
- Enterprise—xSP, Outsource
- Device/OEM Reseller
- Enterprise Solution Providers

Excelsis Group and Lucky have determined that these markets include the following characteristics:

Enterprise

Once evangelized, large and distributed enterprises will adopt Lucky solutions. Enterprises with large, complex sell-side distribution, service and member channels will be among the earliest adopters of Lucky solutions for the collaboration and productivity benefits that strengthen their channel relationships.

Total cost of ownership (TCO) benefits will also play into their longer-term strategic decisions. The downside is that selling to large enterprises involves sales hurdles that include architecture and standards committees, and previous investments that may delay the early adoption of Lucky solutions. Each segment has a distributed member base and the need to share information assets.

Application Service Providers (ASPs) and portal players will become increasingly interested in Lucky's applications. Initial successes may occur with vertical executive dashboards, business applications and content delivery services that focus on segments such as distant learning and customer service. Leading portal players will adopt Lucky-like elements to increase the stickiness of their sites. ASPs will also adopt Lucky-like applications to increase their competitive advantage.

Device OEM/Reseller

National and regional device manufacturers and resellers would benefit from providing their customers with private-labeled business intelligence solutions.

Solution Provider

Independent software vendors, developers and industry solution providers with expertise in vertical segments such as capital goods manufacturing will benefit by providing Lucky-enhanced solutions. To be ultimately successful, Lucky will need to develop an early adopter following in this segment. There is also an opportunity to adopt a Linux-oriented following in the server operating system segment, as previously discussed.

Internet-based Business Intelligence Adoption

Our findings are consistent with analyst predictions that Internet-based business intelligence deployment will occur in phases. The timing of these phases will be influenced both by the availability of appropriate technology and by the availability of experience in developing and deploying associated Internet services.

Open standards will continue to form a foundation for Internet services through which potential benefits such as mobile device access may be enabled. Due to its open architecture, Lucky is therefore well positioned to benefit and has a unique opportunity to accelerate these phases in key segments.

Buyer Profiles

This chart is used to contrast the abilities of Lucky and its competition to satisfy buyer values in key segments. The Relative Value Proposition of each company is derived from the following formula:

Relative Value Proposition = Buyer Value Weight * Value Delivered.

The scores for each company are then used to assess and compare overall capabilities. For instance, an enterprise buyer assigns a high value weight to Channel Access (5). Lucky correspondingly delivers a high degree of satisfaction and capability in meeting that demand (5). Therefore, the Relative Value Proposition is 5 * 5 = 25.

Buyer Value Weight by Primary Segment	Relative Value Proposition = Value Weight * Value Delivered			
	Lucky	Old Blue	Macro soft	Moon Soft
Enterprise				
Channel Access: 5	25	15	10	20
Low Cost of Applications: 4	20	8	8	12
Open Standards: 4	12	20	20	12
Quality Service: 4	8	20	16	16
Sub-Total	65	63	54	60
Solution Provider				
Channel Access: 5	25	15	10	20
Low Cost of Applications: 3	15	6	6	9
Open Standards: 4	20	16	12	16
Quality Service: 3	6	15	12	12
Sub-Total	66	52	40	57

Value Weight and Value Delivered Scale: 5=High, 3=Average, 1=Low

We can see from the Relative Value Proposition sub-totals that Lucky is indeed uniquely positioned to meet the needs of these diverse segments. The scores indicate that Lucky fares relatively well in three of these four areas:

- Channel Access—Information assets are available to anyone, anywhere, anytime, using any device.
- Low Cost of Applications—Initial software license, upgrade, maintenance and setup fees are low. Expenses associated with ongoing maintenance are low.
- Open Standards—The importance of establishing a world-class, next generation computing architecture upon which to build and integrate.
- Quality Service—High quality service includes pre-sale, implementation and post-sale (e.g., help desk, user groups) service.

Marketscape Segmentation Map

This chart compares Lucky and the competitors analyzed in this study along two important axes: completeness of solution and TCO benefits.

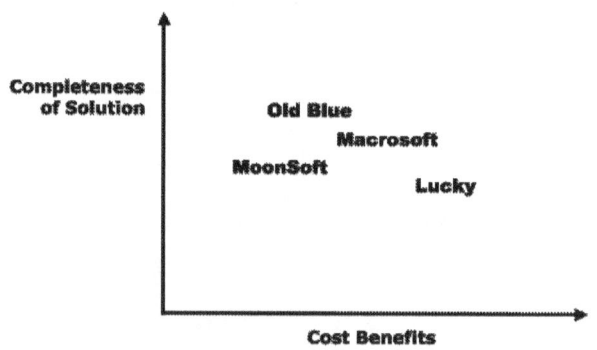

Marketscape Segmentation Map

It is essential for Lucky to develop a complete message hierarchy that addresses the company's unique capabilities in order to distance itself from other vendors. It is also important for a whole product offering to be established as early as possible, to effectively compete with those companies that are already in existence and are more mature.

Dimensional Entry Comparison

Lucky solutions can benefit organizations in almost any industry. However, for Lucky to be successful in the near-term, the company should concentrate its precious resources on those segments that will reap the most immediate benefit, with the least amount of cost and resistance.

The enterprise-related segments should continue to yield the most near-term benefit. Not only does Lucky have experience in this arena, but its solutions are also uniquely capable of solving critical issues that are relevant in the segment.

Dimensional Entry Comparison

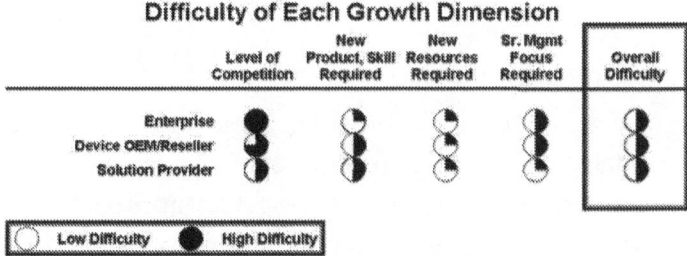

Dimensional Growth Comparison

Based on our research, enterprise segments clearly offer the best near-term opportunity for Lucky. Penetrating the commercial enterprise market will be challenging, but the rewards are significant. Analyst reports indicate that Internet services will continue to make inroads, particularly in the more mature enterprise markets.

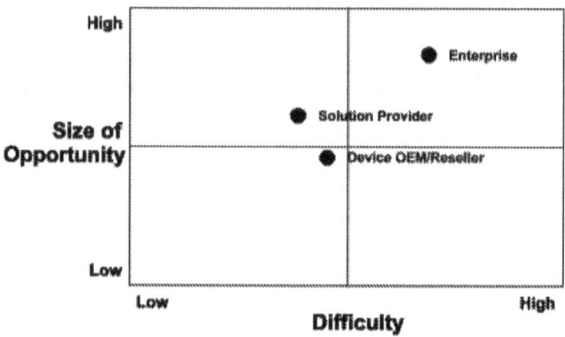

Dimensional Growth Compared

Growth Opportunity Assessment

Bowling Alley with Hub and Spoke Model

Utilizing a combination of "bowling alley" and "hub and spoke" expansion models, Lucky will gain significant re-use and leverage from its sales and marketing efforts. The bowling alley approach initially targets the segments that will yield the greatest penetration and profit, and then leverages the customers, experience and programs to penetrate other segments.

When used in combination, the hub and spoke approach can generate significant viral marketing results, as related segments and suppliers to a Lucky-penetrated segment begin to adopt Lucky's solutions. This model therefore utilizes a serious "reference-selling" approach, and therefore relies on cost-effective sales and marketing programs for support. The company will also be able to effectively cross-sell into these segments as it introduces new solutions.

An important underlying strategy that will become more apparent in the Channel Platform phase

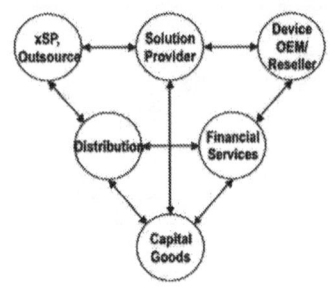

Bowling Alley Expansion Model

Hub and Spoke Strategy Leverages References and Cross Selling

is the need to reach some level of critical mass in the Device OEM/Reseller and Solution Provider markets. While these wins will not realize as much near-term revenue as the direct sales efforts, the long-term value is that an alliance of Macrosoft foes could align around a common cause—Lucky! Secondly, there is ample opportunity for a substantial recurring revenue annuity with this early seeding strategy.

Competitive Assessment Summary

Excelsis Group has prepared detailed competitive analyses along with this competitive assessment summary matrix. In doing so, we have assigned tangible scores to otherwise intangible information. This chart compares Lucky's core competencies and capabilities with representative competitors in key segments.

Dimensions	Lucky	Old Blue	Macro soft	Sun Soft
Business				
Financials	1	4	5	3
Customer Base	1	5	5	4
Marketing				
Messages	2	5	5	4
Brand Value	1	5	5	4
Market Potential	5	5	5	5
Sales/Channels				
Revenue	2	4	5	3
Direct	2	5	5	5
Indirect	2	5	5	4
Solution				
Technology	5	4	3	3
Products	4	5	4	3
Services	1	5	3	4
Price	5	2	3	2
Total	31	54	53	44

Scale: 5=High, 3=Average, 1=Low

From this simple depiction, we can see that Lucky's relative strengths are its superior technology, products and price. Relatively speaking, the company also has many weaknesses.

Competitive Assessment

Information used to produce this Marketscape Platform was obtained from industry analyst groups, industry periodicals and portals, company SEC filings and Web sites, and Lucky internal interviews and sources. Contact Excelsis Group for detailed competitive analysis reports.

Channel Platform

Services

Identify the direct and indirect channel alternatives, complete with significant revenue and expense considerations, to reach the most attractive market segment opportunities. Define and document the sales and marketing models to support these channels, and the whole product requirements for each phase.

Deliverables

- Recommend appropriate channel models for key segments.
- Define the "whole product" requirements to support each model.
- Define market entry models which include characteristics such as entry and growth considerations, and channel strategies and programs.

Macro Channel Model

Based on the initial segments that Excelsis Group identified in the Marketscape Platform, the following macro go-to-market channel model should be considered by Lucky. This chart identifies the channel member categories that should be developed to dominate each of the respective segments, which are comprised of paying customers.

Target Segment	Lucky Direct Sales	Lucky Business Development	System Integrator	Value-Added Reseller
Enterprise	•		•	•
Device OEM/Reseller		•		
Solution Provider		•		

Considering that this is a working document, Excelsis Group expects that Lucky will revise this chart repeatedly, along with the entire platform, as the company evolves. However, this initial view of the channel provides insight for management to determine where resources should be allocated to achieve desired growth objectives.

Channel Definitions

While this Channel Platform depicts a global view of Lucky's go-to-market strategy, the reader should note that securing experienced channel partners is absolutely essential for Lucky in non-domestic markets. Following are brief definitions of each channel member:

- Lucky Direct—The Lucky function that sells Lucky solutions directly to the end customer.
- Lucky Business Development—The "Lucky indirect" function that enlists independent third-party organizations to resell Lucky products to end customers, and includes system integrators and value-added resellers.
- System Integrator—This includes "Big Five" system vendors and independents that provide professional services to apply, migrate and integrate technology into business processes.
- Value-Added Reseller—This includes resellers that are usually not storefront operations and typically act as consultants to clients. To qualify as a VAR, a reseller must have developed or configured some type of solution that is targeted at a particular market or offer significant integration and post-sale expertise to the customer.

Lucky will need to determine specific performance criteria for its channel program, and determine the specific value-add benefits (e.g., enterprise experience and relationships, Web services integration, Linux) that each prospective VAR can deliver before admitting them into the program. Each VAR will then need to deliver "value" and achieve revenue objectives to stay in the program. Conversely, Lucky will need to develop and maintain a high quality channel program that truly empowers VARs and integrators.

Channel Penetration Model

Utilizing a focused frontal assault strategy with Lucky's direct sales organization and high-level system integration efforts, this model is supplemented by a flanking maneuver that leverages reseller and other channel relationships.

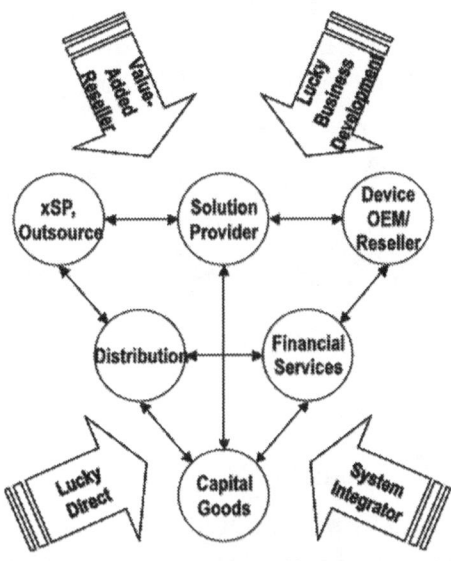

It is essential for Lucky to promote its early "direct sale" wins, which will support the rapid adoption of Lucky solutions by additional customers, segments and partners. This reference-based "viral marketing" approach will result in the most cost-effective use of Lucky resources to achieve the desired revenue objectives. This channel model is designed to maximize revenue while minimizing channel conflict and duplicate effort.

Viral Marketing

As discussed, this approach is extremely cost-effective, and should ultimately result in wildfires of demand whereby communities with many thousands and even millions of users begin to evangelize and adopt Lucky solutions. A viral marketing approach can be extremely cost-effective when it leverages reference-based selling practices throughout the process. Lucky solutions—unlike Macrosoft solutions—are not constrained by desktop deployment. Without desktops or geographic borders, the potential is immense.

This viral adoption model holds tremendous promise in the segments that have been identified by Excelsis Group. For instance, large manufacturers with complex sell-side channels will adopt Lucky solutions—a division at a time—and will then serve as references and case studies for further market penetration within the channel itself, and laterally to suppliers, other related businesses and even competitors. This scenario is depicted in the following diagram:

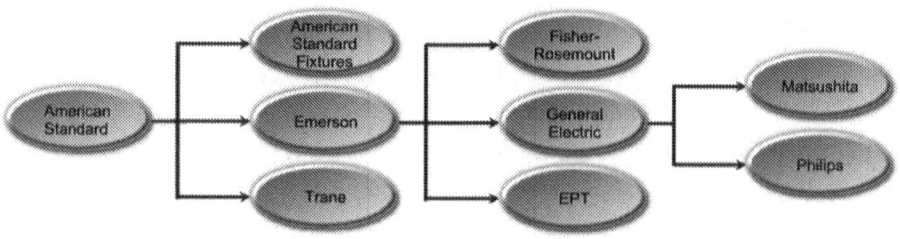

Sales Roadmap

Lucky has adopted the following three-phase sales roadmap to identify, qualify and close business, and support customers. Each phase includes simple yet essential best practices, tool requirements and deliverables.

Phase I: Pre-Qualify Opportunities

Lucky has determined that a telemarketing operation would dramatically increase the quality of leads that are generated for the sales force. Telemarketing representatives will operate from a campaign schedule, and will be armed with a battery of scripts, letters and marketing material to aid them. They will in turn utilize online services, provide initial literature fulfillment and generate pre-qualified leads.

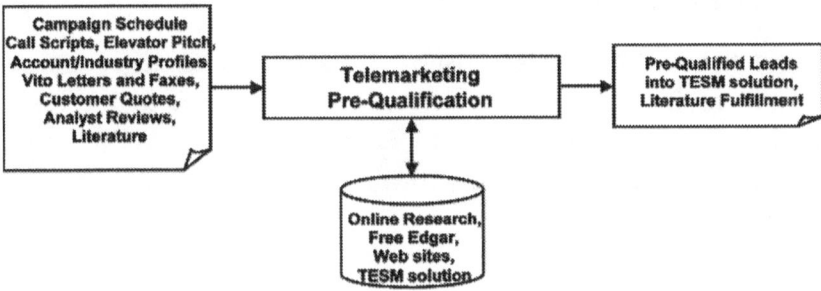

Phase II: Qualify and Close Business

Lucky's sales force will then further qualify each opportunity and move each prospect through four stages. As each opportunity progresses, its probability of closure increases from 25 to 90%, unless it is eliminated from the pipeline. Lucky determined early in its planning process that it would utilize technology to increase the effectiveness and efficiency of its sales force. This will be discussed further in the Technology Platform section.

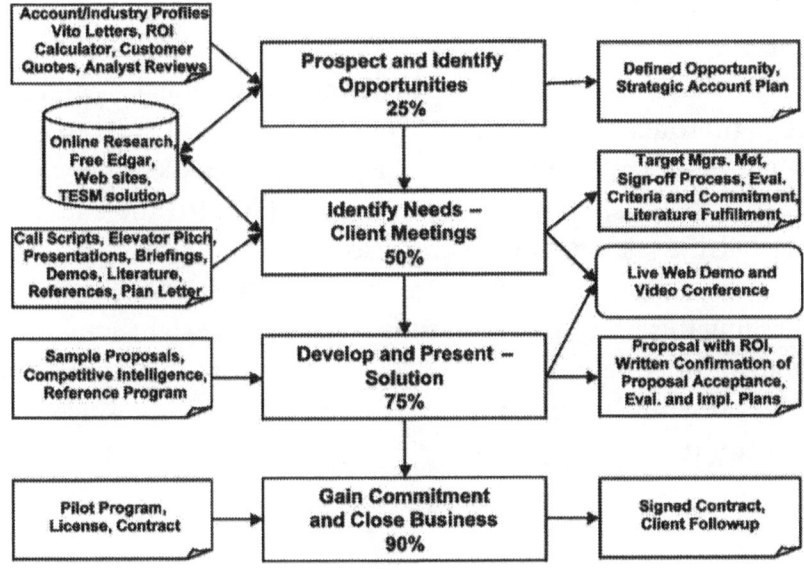

Phase III: Post-Sales Support

Once a prospect becomes a customer, the post-sales support organization is formally engaged. The function of this team is to develop and maintain satisfied customers. Lucky is confident that this investment will generate additional business through cross-selling opportunities, new business referrals, etc.

Sales Cycle Time Reduction

Finally, Excelsis Group has the following recommendations for Lucky to reduce from 4-6 months its average sales cycle time to approximately two months.

- Sales Roadmap—Once agreed-upon, sales management and representatives should adhere to Lucky's sales roadmap and an accompanying sales reporting process.
- Sales Education—Each sales and channel professional should complete a thorough Lucky Sales Orientation workshop prior to engaging in sales. This training should include modules that address industry verticals, competitive solutions, Selling 101 the Lucky Way, and available sales and marketing resources.
- Reference Program—Each sales representative should consider leveraging this program as a closing vehicle in the right situation.
- Executive Briefing Program—Lucky should invest in a simple, high-quality briefing program to maximize this critical touch point opportunity.

Significantly reducing the current cycle time is highly probable if these initiatives are acted upon.

Lucky Marketing Organization

In order to maximize revenue opportunities, Excelsis Group recommends that Lucky work toward developing a complete marketing structure that includes public relations, marketing communications, product marketing, product management and telemarketing. Based on our understanding, this model leverages personnel investments that Lucky has made and it further positions the company to expand in the coming quarters and years.

Revenue Expectations

During our initial meetings, Lucky management articulated the following three-year goals for the company:

- Achieve critical mass in the enterprise marketplace by capturing 30% of the Fortune 500,
- Establish further inroads in Western Europe and Asia, and
- Realize $250 million in revenue.

Revenue Growth Strategies

Based on the analysis that has been completed in the Performance Marketing Platform, and the direction from Lucky management, Excelsis Group has documented growth projection scenarios in the following charts.

Beginning with its most significant sales and marketing investment in the identified enterprise segments, Lucky will ultimately diversify its efforts to achieve a more balanced revenue stream.

These efforts will capitalize on the reference-based go-to-market approach and growing market demands that were previously discussed, to achieve the outcome that is depicted in this chart:

Growth by Industry

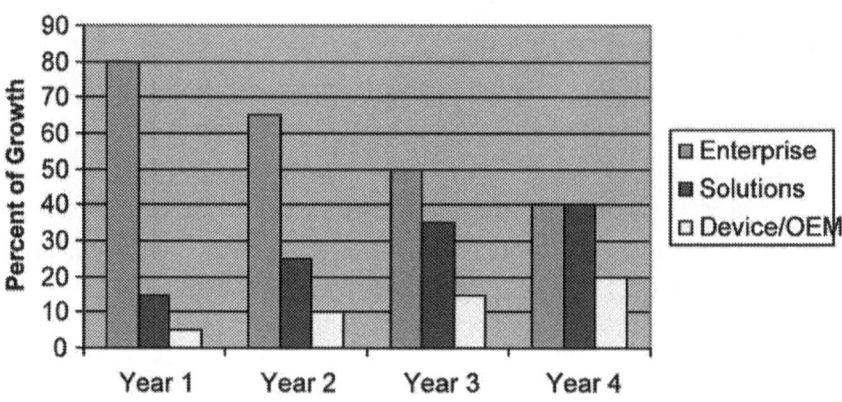

While Lucky is continuing to make inroads in Western Europe, the company will need to ramp up significantly to meet the rigorous demands of a discriminating international marketplace. These demands include investments in localized product, regional facilities, personnel, etc.

Following is a conservative depiction of Lucky's geographic growth model, which assumes minimal investment in product (e.g., double-byte enablement, language localization) and local sales resources (i.e., Lucky would rely primarily on partners/resellers).

Growth by Geography

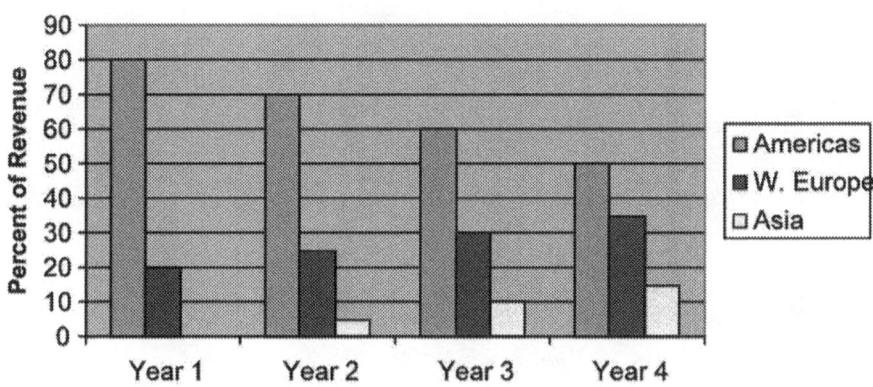

Should Lucky decide to grow more aggressively, it will need to factor into its international expansion plans the fact that U.S. sales currently take 4-6 months and are likely to require additional time abroad. An aggressive model would also assume that rapid progress will be made toward meeting the product needs of individual markets, and building significant regional sales and marketing operations overseas.

The following model assumes that Lucky will realize 50 percent of its revenue from indirect channels by Year 4. Note that it relies primarily on an aggressive, direct selling organization to fuel the company's expansion plans.

Growth by Channel

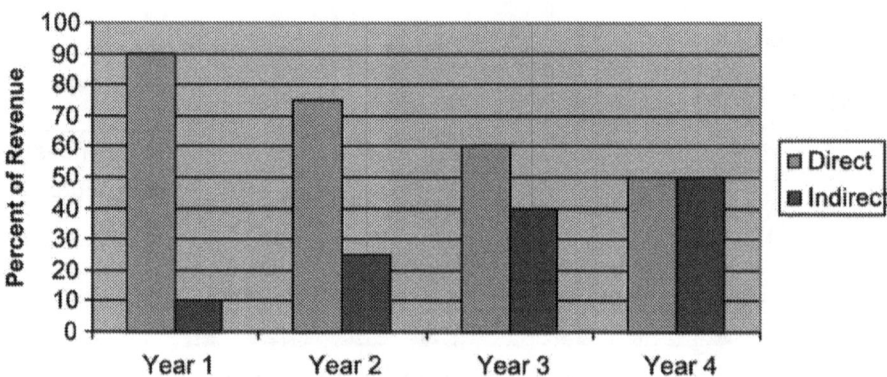

The above growth analyses underscore the need to develop a diversified go-to-market sales and marketing team that meets the needs of buyers in multiple industries and geographies.

In doing so, it is important for Lucky to offer a world-class partner program to eliminate false starts in this area—timing is critical, and there are too many alternatives for prospective business partners and customers. It is also important for Lucky to develop a marketing machine that can be easily leveraged on a worldwide basis. For instance, each message, brochure and program should be created with a global application in mind.

Whole Product Components

In order to be most effective and successful, this channel model requires corporate commitment to each direct sales employee and indirect partner, which requires extending functionality beyond the actual core products.

Large enterprise customers and their partners have grown accustomed to mature, highly developed whole product offerings. Therefore, to be sure that Lucky is always in a target prospect's purchase consideration set, Lucky solutions should include the following whole product attributes for relevant channel members:

Whole Product Checklist

Software

- Production-ready (defect-free)
- Complete packaging
- Easy to install

Documentation

- Complete portfolio

Consulting

- Installation packages
- Quick start packages
- Integration and tuning packages
- Lucky consulting bench strength
- Consulting methodology
- Implementation advice
- Certification program

Standards and Procedures

- Open architecture
- Maintenance best practices
- Integration best practices

Post-Sale Support

- Help desk support
- Maintenance program
- User groups and networks
- Restricted web site

Education

- Direct sales
- Indirect sales
- Implementation
- Administration

Pre-Sale Support

- Price models
- Price protection plans
- Pre-sales support
- Installation and trial support
- Proposal and contract support
- Lead distribution and tracking
- Financial assistance for partners
- Commission models
- Tiered partner program elements

Channel Support

- Partner brochures and materials
- Partner web links
- Co-marketing programs
- Lucky certified solution program
- Lucky developer connection program
- Partner network

Additional Hardware and Software

- Bundled packages

Should Lucky not be prepared at this time to meet or support certain criteria, the company should factor this into its evaluation of the proper timing to pursue specific channel opportunities and expansion strategies.

Brand Platform

Services

Research, analyze and develop a brand platform for Lucky, complete with brand positioning, message hierarchies and brand expansion strategies.

Deliverables

- Competitive brand positioning analysis—Review of how Lucky and its competitors are positioning themselves in the marketplace.
- Competitive brand experience map—A comparative analysis of the competitive brand positioning mapped by each Lucky market segment and their desired experience with the brand.
- Brand message hierarchy—Market category, positioning statement, winning value proposition and supporting statements that Lucky will take to the marketplace.
- Brand expansion strategies that take the company to the next level.

Competitive Brand Positioning Analysis

The following chart encapsulates the marketing messages that are being directed to business and technology buyers.

Company	Business Messages	Technology Messages
Lucky Software	• Economical, low total cost of ownership • Supports access for all classes of users – novice, power and executive	• Reduces hardware requirements • Reduces software license fees • Increases productivity • Integrates into existing platforms • Easy to administer • Scales to support many users
Old Blue	• Using its Web service-enabled business intelligence solutions, customers gain the highest level of business advantage	• Build, deploy and integrate high-performance business applications using open standards • Runs across multiple platforms • Extend what you have and run where you want
Macrosoft	• Empower people through information access any time, any place, on any device • Solutions that enable customers to act on information wherever and whenever they need it	• Focus on smart clients – fat and thin • Technologies for connecting worlds of information, people, systems and devices • Web services are building-blocks that connect and create a network of interconnected services and resources
MoonSoft	• Ensure that information services are available to anyone, anywhere, anytime, using any device • Low total cost of ownership	• Full featured functionality for a compelling price • Doesn't lock you into a single environment • Open, flexible developer environment • Open, non-proprietary standards • Centralization of management and information reduces costs

From the above chart, it is evident that each company is making similar claims. Lucky will need to be consistent and somewhat dramatic in order to gain the attention of the broad market. Old Blue, Macrosoft and MoonSoft are able to rely on their brand names and leverage their impressive customer bases.

Competitive Brand Experience Map

Drawing from the information that was gathered in the Marketscape Platform phase, this chart identifies buyer values that are being addressed—to some degree—by respective solutions. The purpose of this chart is not to evaluate how well each company satisfies individual needs, but instead to identify key messages with which each company goes-to-market.

Buyer Value	Lucky	Old Blue	Macro soft	MoonSoft
Channel Access	√	√	√	√
Low Cost of Applications	√			√
Open Standards	√	√	√	√
Quality Service				

While most of the companies are touting "anytime, anywhere" access, Lucky's messages and value propositions will be most unique and compelling when they emphasize the low total cost of ownership for its business intelligence applications.

Lucky Brand Hierarchy

By adopting a "Lucky" product name prefix, the company can leverage its existing trademark investment (e.g., legal and branding). This further enables Lucky to benefit from the promotion of a single corporate brand identity, rather than having to invest in the development and publicity of multiple disparate brands. Excelsis Group has prepared the following chart, which depicts the proposed product and service name hierarchy:

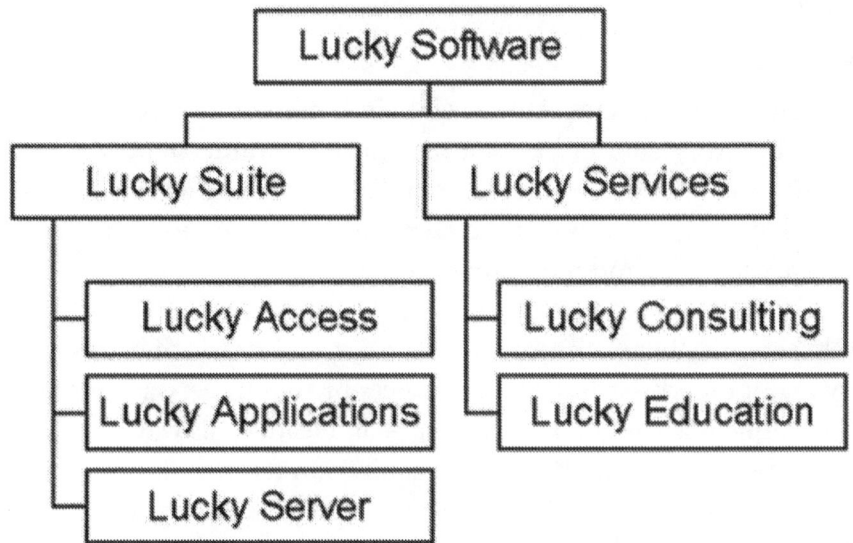

Brand Message Hierarchy

To reiterate the vision from the Marketscape Platform:

> *Lucky's vision is to ensure that information assets*
> *are accessible from anywhere on the planet.*

Slogan

After extensive market testing, the following slogan is being presented for consideration:

> *Software for the Good Fortune 500.*

This slogan personalizes the unique possibilities that Lucky solutions afford large growing enterprises, while personalizing the message with the subtle use humor.

Message Matrix

It is important for Lucky to develop and build upon a common storyline. This story should be exciting, simple to understand and offer great promise. Based on our research, it should include business and technical messages, supporting statements and evidence, and should permeate each sales and marketing program.

Excelsis Group recommends that Lucky seriously consider adopting a Web Services theme throughout its sales and marketing programs. Every major enterprise has a Web Services project underway and Lucky is in a unique position to benefit from—and lead—this wave.

This strategy will help the sales organization to open doors, and will also enable Lucky to grab significant media, industry analyst and investor attention. Finally, this strategy will surely have a positive impact on Lucky's international and channel expansion efforts where Web Services are in equally high demand.

Finally, the Web Services segment satisfies Excelsis Group's criteria for adopting a market category. Ideally, the desired segment will be:

- An appealing market that is easy to understand,
- A growing market,
- A large market, and
- A market in which you can dominate.

Buyer Values in Balance

Lucky has a unique opportunity to communicate a concise set of complementary messages, which speak volumes to CxO leadership across business and technology disciplines.

The following message matrix articulates the primary solution level messages for senior business and technology buyers. These messages serve as the baseline for quickly developing consistent sales and marketing programs and assets. This important matrix is to be used by all marketing, telemarketing and sales professionals, and shared with channel partners.

Lucky Software Message Matrix

Target Business Profile

Enterprise

- In an identified target segment
- Large, complex sell-side channel with distributors or service centers or 30,000+ employees or members
- Price sensitive
- Has immediate problem or a business intelligence or Web Services project
- Dealing with a decision maker

Valid Business Messages

Saves me money!

- Lucky saves me money. I increase my productivity and the value of information across my extended enterprise networks.

Empowers everyone!

- Lucky solutions empower everyone to securely access corporate information assets.

Includes feature-rich applications!

- Lucky's feature-rich suite of business applications provide instant access—anywhere, anytime, using any device.

Transforms my business!

- Lucky solutions transform business models by adapting to your business.

Valid Technology Messages

Saves me money!

- Lucky saves me money. I eliminate significant expenses, increase my productivity and agility, and the value of information across my enterprise networks.

Simplifies my life!

- Lucky's architecture enables me to consolidate and centralize people, skills and information technology assets.

Improves my service levels!

- Allows me to provide consistent, excellent service anywhere in the world—with near-zero administration!

Features a next generation service platform!

- Lucky scales to support all of my users, supports and co-exists with other applications and is platform independent.

Brand Expansion Strategies

As Lucky continues to expand its product line—via breadth and depth—it should consider the following options:

- Adding to the suite—An example is to include collaboration and groupware solutions that can benefit Lucky Suite users.
- Double-byte support—A requirement in Asia's largest markets.
- Linux support—As discussed, this is a major opportunity for Lucky.
- Services—There will continue to be a requirements for numerous Lucky Service offerings—from product training to consulting packages—that can be developed to increase customer and partner satisfaction.

Communications Platform

Services

Develop an integrated marketing plan for each primary stakeholder audience, and provide strategic counsel and input to properly reintroduce Lucky to the market.

Deliverables

- Marketing plan—Identify marketing opportunities and make specific strategic and tactical suggestions across the various elements of the marketing mix.

Condensed Marketing Plan Overview

As discussed previously in this Performance Marketing Platform, Lucky Software is adopting a reference-based, industry "bowling alley" approach. As such, this Communications Platform targets stakeholders (e.g., enterprise buyers, media and industry analysts, tradeshows, etc.) in the capital goods, distribution, financial service and xSP industries. Regardless of the vehicles that are used, disciplined and cost-effective target marketing practices should be utilized.

Secondly, as is often the case with emerging high technology companies, Lucky has not allocated a substantial amount of money toward marketing. This plan therefore focuses on high-impact telemarketing, direct marketing, public relations and sales enablement programs as opposed to expensive, broad-based, image-building advertising programs.

Finally, Lucky is adhering to the sales channel that was discussed in the Channel Platform. Initially, the marketing organization is focused primarily on supporting the direct sales force, with less emphasis on the indirect channels.

Marketing Production Schedule

The Marketing Production Schedule is a best practice tool that enables Performance Marketing professionals to present a complete 12-18 month marketing plan at-a-glance in a simple spreadsheet format. Following is a sampling of the marketing functions that Lucky Software is monitoring via its schedule:

Product Marketing
- Marketing Strategy
- Sales Programs and Tools
- Product Launch

Product Management
- Product Requirements

Public Relations
- PR Strategy
- Press Releases
- Media Relations
- Analyst Relations
- Customer Relations
- Employee Relations

- Community Relations
- Investor Relations
- Channel Relations
- Speaker's Bureau
- Communications Kit

Marketing Communications
- Communication Strategy
- Direct Marketing
- Web Marketing
- Advertising
- Collateral
- Multimedia
- Event Marketing
- Employee Events
- Customer Events

Telemarketing
- Direct Sales
- Channel Sales

Author's note: A formal, rolling budget that includes program, operational and fixed expenses should accompany the Marketing Production Schedule. Due to brevity and relevance considerations, it has not been included in this case study.

Technology Platform

Services

Make strategic recommendations for the implementation of an integrated technology platform that meets the near- and long-term needs of the sales and marketing organizations.

Deliverables

- Conduct a formal analysis and establish the requirements for meeting the needs of the sales and marketing organizations.
- Survey the market and recommend solutions that best meet these requirements.

Objectives

After reviewing Lucky Software's objectives and gathering requirements from its executive team, Excelsis Group has determined that a technology-enabled sales and marketing (TESM) solution would best meet the company's near-term needs, while establishing a platform upon which to add customer service capabilities in the future.

Senior management has articulated that the primary objectives for implementing a Technology Platform are to:

- Generate sales leads and increase revenue.
- Help create a strong, high value brand.
- Improve customer satisfaction.
- Enhance partner relationships.
- Attract and retain talented people.

Requirements

Given Lucky Software's refined go-to-market strategy and limited marketing budget, Excelsis Group suggests that a telemarketing program can provide high value, low cost-per-lead results if implemented properly. This is especially true when integrated with other functions of the sales and marketing mix such as direct and channel sales, direct marketing, seminars and events, and advertising.

Functional Requirements

Ultimately, the TESM platform should allow sales and marketing personnel to accomplish the following high-level functional objectives:

- Capture research, and customer and prospect contact information in a central database.
- Provide outbound telemarketing call support to follow-up on seminars, maintain conversations and relationships with prospects, cold call from lists, profile prospects and transition qualified leads.
- Provide inbound call support to respond to inquiries that have been generated through other marketing programs.
- Generate pipeline and forecast reports that reflect Lucky Software's defined Sales Roadmap methodology.
- Provide a blend of sales and marketing functionality in a base package, with room to grow.
- Conduct online research for specific segments and prospects, to generate marketing lists, profile companies, size market segments, etc.
- Provide professional videoconference capabilities to conduct cost-effective remote sales meetings.

Additional Considerations

In addition to the stated functional requirements, Lucky management has expressed the need to enable the organization for growth, build long-standing relationships with customers and work within short-term timing and budget considerations.

Senior management is also in agreement that a somewhat generic, yet flexible, hosted application service provider (ASP) solution would be preferable if it does not require additional hardware or personnel investments. Since Lucky is an emerging market company, your internal IT department is reportedly not prepared to implement and maintain your system.

You expressed the need to begin using the system near-term and stated that you cannot afford to wait several months to begin using it. Ideally, you would begin to use the system within days—not weeks or months.

You prefer to adopt a solution that offers self-directed "just in time" online education, since you are not planning to develop and offer classroom and/or online TESM training for sales professionals and partners.

Finally, you have expressed the desire to work with an established company that has solid customer references and proven, market-ready solutions.

Recommendations

After extensive review of Lucky management's requirements and the preceding Performance Marketing Platform findings, Excelsis Group has surveyed the market and recommends that Lucky adopt a hosted ASP solution, and online research and videoconference services.

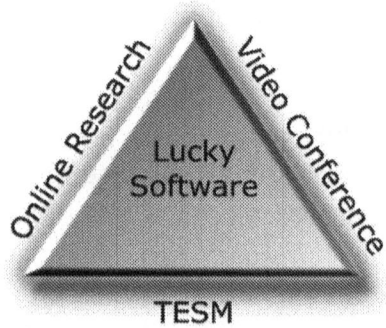

As of this writing, Salesforce.com and Outtask.com are ASP industry leaders whose TESM solutions should be considered in the evaluation process. WebEx and Microsoft NetMeeting video conference solutions should also be reviewed, as should Hoovers, D&B and OneSource online research services.

The process for selecting the solution that most closely meets Lucky's diverse needs should include the establishment of a cross-functional evaluation team, which is headed by an individual who is empowered to make decisions for the company.

This evaluation team should prepare and distribute a formal request for proposal document and a workgroup calendar that meets Lucky's requirements.

Product Launch Checklist

Following is a generic, yet comprehensive, product launch checklist that can be customized for specific industries, solutions and circumstances. Each task should have an owner/responsible party, begin and end date, and critical path association (if applicable). This checklist should be maintained in electronic form by the product launch manager.

Product Launch Operations

- Establish a Cross Functional Team (CFT).
- Identify a CFT leader.
- Publish CFT goals.

Whole Product Creation

- Conduct a strategic assessment.
- Define and document the product positioning.
- Define product requirements.
- Develop a marketing plan.
- Conduct an analyst working session.
- Prepare a marketing launch budget.
- Conduct a product name trademark search.
- Apply for a product name trademark application.
- Select a final product name.
- Create a product license agreement.
- Migrate development code to quality assurance (QA).
- Migrate code from QA to product manufacturing.
- Complete the product installation setup.

- Create an on-line Help facility.
- Complete the beta program process.
- Create/update manuals for general availability (GA).
- Develop a trial kit for GA.
- Define a product upgrade kit.
- Update education courseware.

Beta Process

- Define product quality measurement criteria.
- Communicate new product features internally.
- Develop test plans.
- Recruit beta customers.
- Prepare a site verification checklist.
- Create/update manuals for beta customers.
- Duplicate beta test manuals.
- Announce the beta program.
- Provide weekly beta status reports.
- Support beta customers.

Pricing and Finance

- Develop product pricing model(s).
- Develop financial model(s).
- Identify enterprise/site license requirements.
- Publish maintenance/support options.
- Develop consulting services pricing model(s).
- Prepare/amend product licenses.

Public Relations

- Determine goals and deliverables.
- Identify and train key spokespersons.
- Produce communication materials.
- Prepare press release or other targeted activity.
- Contact customer references for analysts/press.

- Conduct analyst conference calls and visits.
- Conduct press conference calls and visits.
- Develop six-month communications plans.

Communications

- Announce GA status.
- Produce brochures, case studies and demos.
- Design product packaging and inserts.
- Initiate advertising.
- Initiate direct mail.
- Initiate internal publications/newsletters.
- Initiate external publications/journals.
- Update on-line services.
- Update event booth graphics.
- Initiate executive breakfasts.
- Initiate road shows.
- Initiate trade show participation.

Sales, Channel and Services Enablement

- Publish direct and indirect model(s).
- Publish services model(s).
- Produce sales strategy sheets.
- Produce quick reference sheets.
- Produce fact sheets.
- Produce audio tapes.
- Produce product demo.
- Produce overview presentation w/script.
- Produce product futures presentation w/script.
- Produce telesales script(s).
- Publish trial/product evaluation agreement.
- Publish detailed competitive analysis.
- Publish competitive pricing matrix.

- Publish customer reference sites.
- Notify sales.
- Notify partners.
- Notify services.
- Update the sales intranet.
- Update the channel extranet.

International

- Define international product requirements.
- Define international sales requirements.
- Define international marketing requirements.
- Forward beta internal/external announcements.
- Forward GA internal/external announcements.
- Distribute marketing plans and programs.
- Assist regional offices with marketing campaigns.

Training

- Develop education classes.
- Train outside sales.
- Train telesales.
- Train sales support.
- Train customer support.
- Training consulting.

Order Fulfillment

- Publish product descriptions.
- Publish pricing/maintenance options.
- Assign password keys.
- Publish a Bill of Materials.
- Enter documentation into the order entry system.
- Enter media into the order entry system.
- Publish a product set definition.
- Estimate the number of manuals and media needed.

- Document bin locations for product components.
- Process a test order.
- Publish the availability date.
- Set up a trial version.

Manufacturing/Packaging

- Produce product manuals.
- Produce product packaging.
- Duplicate media.
- Publish cover letter to users.
- Verify Bill of Materials.
- Produce a trial kit.
- Notify Distribution of beta availability.
- Notify Distribution of GA availability.

Distribution

- Assemble the product kit.
- Shrink wrap the product kit.
- Ship to clients.
- Track and reorder inventory.
- Publish the password distribution method.
- Inform distributors of the past version disposition.
- Notify product marketing that the product is ready.

Follow-up

- Post-release clarification and information.
- Post-release product launch plan evaluation.
- Post-release marketing plan evaluation.

Marketing Assessment Questionnaire

This questionnaire may be used during initial management meetings to initiate a Performance Marketing Platform engagement. Chances are good that the answers will vary widely—especially as they relate to the all-important elevator speech—which supports the need for the marketing best practices that are described in this text.

General Business

- Ideally, what will be different about your business in 12 months (i.e., your beachhead objectives, etc.)?
- Who are your primary competitors today? In 12 months?
- How are you better?
- Describe your customer base (e.g., media references, number, by industry, etc.).

General Business: The Elevator Speech

- What are the top differentiators for your business?
- What are the top differentiators for your products/services?
- For whom does your elevator speech resonate (business and person)?
- Why does it resonate?
- Who are your top competitors and why are you better?

Marketing

- What are your overall marketing objectives (e.g., brand development, brand awareness, category development, lead generation, sales and channel enablement, etc.)?
- What are your current initiatives by discipline (i.e., strategic marketing, public relations, advertising, Web, direct and event marketing, etc.)?
- What additional initiatives do you anticipate over the next 3-4 quarters?
- Who are your buyers and what are your unique selling propositions for each?
- Who are the additional audiences that you would like to influence?
- Who are your spokespersons, by function?
- How is your marketing department organized?
- How is the marketing budget allocated?

Sales

- Describe your sales organization (e.g., inside sales, outside sales, indirect partners, geographies, etc.).

Development

- What is the release schedule for the next 12 months?

About the Author

Wm. Edward Vesely is the founder of Excelsis Group, a strategic marketing firm that helps high technology companies achieve break-through results and leadership positions. He consults with dozens of corporations and pioneers the use of technology to improve sales and marketing performance.

Mr. Vesely holds bachelor degrees in Journalism and Computer Science from Northern Illinois University, and an MBA in Marketing from DePaul University.

0-595-24690-7

www.ingramcontent.com/pod-product-compliance
Lightning Source LLC
Chambersburg PA
CBHW030803180526
45163CB00003B/1143